DATE DUE			
APR 17 '65			
APR 8 1974			
DEC 7 1976			
DEC 1 8 1976			
AC mar 7 9			
GAYLORD 234			PRINTED IN U.S.A.

THE EARLY MIDDLE AGES

IS VOLUME

76

OF THE

Twentieth Century Encyclopedia of Catholicism

UNDER SECTION

VII

THE HISTORY OF THE CHURCH

IT IS ALSO THE

46TH

VOLUME IN ORDER OF PUBLICATION

Edited by HENRI DANIEL-ROPS of the Académie Française

THE EARLY MIDDLE AGES

By *BERNARD GUILLEMAIN*

Translated from the French by S. TAYLOR

HAWTHORN BOOKS · PUBLISHERS · *New York*

First Edition, July, 1960
Second Printing, November, 1962

NIHIL OBSTAT

Adrianus van Vliet, S.T.D.

Censor Deputatus

IMPRIMATUR

E. Morrogh Bernard

Vicarius Generalis

Westmonasterii, die I APRILIS MCMLX

CONTENTS

THE EARLY MIDDLE AGES

PART I

CHRISTIANITY AND THE FORMS OF CHRISTENDOM AT THE BEGINNING OF THE ELEVENTH CENTURY

CHAPTER I

THE SPREAD OF THE GOSPEL

At the point where this history begins, a thousand years had elapsed since the Gospel message was proclaimed. We are fully aware of the profound transformations of all kinds that had taken place in the ten centuries preceding the one we are concerned with; we must beware against letting the extreme distance in time blind us to the evolution that marked the first thousand years of Christianity.

THE GEOGRAPHY OF THE CHRISTIAN WORLD

Examination of a map showing the area covered by Christianity at the beginning of the eleventh century reveals two striking facts. The mass of Christian territory is to be found to the north of the Mediterranean, in a strip of land running from Asia Minor in the south-east to Ireland in the north-west, beset by Islam in the south and looking out to the north on to vast spaces whose sparsely scattered inhabitants are still heathen. The sea, around which Christianity spread within the confines of the Roman Empire, had now become a frontier. Islam had overwhelmed Palestine and Syria, had conquered North Africa and the greater part of the Iberian peninsula; Koranic law ran from the plains of the Indus to the estuary of the Tagus. Yet at the same time the Church, having lost basic geographic positions, did not even embrace in one faith all men who believed in redemption through Jesus Christ: in the East there were communities that continued to subscribe to the heresies propounded at the time of the great Christo-logical disputes of the fifth century, and they clung to these views all the more firmly since they had made them the basis of their individual nationalisms in the face of the eastern emperors or the Muslim caliphs: the Armenians, the Jacobites in Syria, the Copts in Egypt and the Ethiopians recognized in Christ only the divine nature despite the condemnation of Monophysitism pronounced at the Council of Chalcedon in 451; the Nestorians, on the other hand, convinced that there were two Persons in the Saviour since in him subsisted divine nature and human nature, formed active groups in Mesopo-tamia and Iran, where they gained entry into the entourage of the caliphs; their religious head, the *catholicos*, by this time installed in Baghdad, supervised the astonishing proselytizing activities, along the caravan routes of central Asia and among the tribes of Turkestan, of missionaries who propagated as far as China a Christian doctrine rejected by the Bishop of Rome and by the Council of Ephesus in the first third of the fifth century!

With the exception of the Anatolian peninsula, the bastions of Christianity were henceforth European: about the year 1000, if the Macedonian dynasty was giving new lustre to the lands of ancient civilization surrounding the Aegean Sea, a second centre of culture was being established in Germany, in the lands between the Meuse and the Elbe which the Carolingians only two centuries earlier had made the centre of gravity of the West and which—preserved by distance from the Norman and Saracen invasions that had devastated the British Isles, the coasts of Frisia, France and Italy—had been saved by the dynasty of the Ottos from the Magyar peril. But, driven to the defensive in the south, Christianity had but lately seen open out before it wide vistas to the north of the old Roman frontiers: beneath the yoke of Islam the ancient patriarchates of Jeru-salem and Alexandria, the religious houses in the Holy Land and Sicily, the Mozarabic groups in Spain, the half-dozen bishoprics that survived in North Africa led a precarious existence; on the other hand, the Church had set about the conquest of the Scandinavians and the Slavs.

By the efforts of German and Anglo-Saxon missionaries, and thanks to the union of England and Denmark under the authority of Canute and the conversions of kings, bishoprics were founded in Jutland, Britain and Scania; the remains of the saintly King Olaf were venerated at Nidaros (Trondhjem), Christianity was proclaimed the official religion of Iceland; and in the course of the eleventh century, through the despatch of itinerant prelates, through the consecration of bishops at Bremen (whose metropolitan laid claim to overriding authority over the northern churches) and through the rapid training of a native priesthood, southern Scandinavia and Iceland were won over to the Christian religion. The Western Empire found itself in contact with the Slavs along the Elbe and the Saale, the mountains of Bohemia, in Carinthia and Istria, while the Eastern Empire encountered them in the Balkans and to the north of the Black Sea; both the Germans and the Greeks had been eager for their conversion for reasons that were not purely missionary. Between the Baltic and the Erzgebirge, among the Wends, the Christian outposts that depended on the recently created archbishopric of Magdeburg hardly went beyond the Elbe and the Saale; but the Czechs, on the other hand, who had been reached in the third quarter of the ninth century by the preaching of the Greek saints Cyril and Methodius, and had later come under German rule, allowed themselves gradually to be converted by their dukes—of whom Wenceslas had been the first to be baptized—and through the action of the bishops of Prague, in dependence on the metropolitan see of Mainz; across the Oder, German troops had penetrated as far as the lands of Prince Mieszko, which at the beginning of the eleventh century adopted the name of "land of the plains", or Poland; the prince, who married a Czech princess, had been baptized in 965, had founded first at Poznan a bishopric attached to Magdeburg, and then in 999 a national metropolitan see at Gniezno; his son, Boleslav the Mighty, obtained the royal title from the pope in 1025. The same favour had recently been granted to Stephen, the leader of the Hungarians established in the central Danubian plain; after hearing preachers from Salzburg, these barbarians, who had spread terror around them, were now embodied in a new ecclesiastical province centred on Gran (Esztergom). These youthful churches could find a bond and an example in their devotion to St Adalbert, the Czech Bishop of Prague and the apostle of the monastic life in Poland and Hungary, who was martyred by the Prussians and buried at Gniezno.

The new kingdom of Hungary separated the northern Slavs from their southern brothers: among the latter only the Croats and Slovenes had accepted the faith of the West; the Serbs and the Bulgarians who, originating in Asia, had rapidly assimilated themselves to the Slavs, had been evangelized by disciples of Cyril and Methodius who had instituted a liturgy in the Slavonic tongue; but the churches had been rapidly brought round to Greek customs. Finally, in the east, the principality of Kiev, made up of the association of Slavonic tribes with Scandinavian merchants who traversed the great plains between the upper Baltic coast and the shores of the Black Sea, had opened its doors to Christianity: a church had been established in Kiev, then about 987 Vladimir—won over, it is said, by the splendour of the Byzantine liturgy—was converted, and had made his subjects bathe in the waters of the Dniepr for the baptism of regeneration; he obtained for Kiev the foundation of a metropolitan see whose first holders were provided by the Greek clergy.

We should beware of seeking to evaluate the dimensions of this Christian world in present-day terms. The most knowledgeable people of those days were the Arabs, profiting as they did from the legacies of Greek science, from the accounts of their travellers and traders; and even they did not imagine that the world extended beyond the equator and the Atlantic Ocean—for them it was confined to the continent of Asia and the two long peninsulas of Europe and North Africa, and even then they were mistaken about the true area of the Asian continent. The Christian, therefore, with his more rudimentary geographical knowledge, was even less likely to have a true idea of the size of the world. Distances were accentuated by the slowness of travel, the dearth of roads, the scattering of communities, natural obstacles and the scarcity of information about any region other than the one in which people lived out their daily lives. The multitude of political divisions, the variety of cultures, the unequal spread of the Gospel message were so many factors making for fragmentation, yet unifying factors existed.

UNIFYING FACTORS

The first of these was belief in the supernatural mission of the Church, depositary of divine grace which she passes on through the sacraments to the faithful, guardian of dogma and of a moral system which are based on divine revelation itself, entrusted with maintaining the worship of the true God and, through her hierarchy instituted by Jesus Christ, bringing men to eternal salvation. Christians, by reason of their baptism, all belonged to a single society, whose direction was claimed by the Bishop of Rome—the successor to the apostle Peter—and whose officers were the bishops. This society was divided into the three great "orders" of clergy, monks and laymen.

It was not only spiritual life that animated this great body, for institutions fashioned its features in space and time, while interchanges of many kinds bore visible witness to its unity. A mosaic of dioceses, grouped into provinces, covered the lands where the Gospel had been preached; the creation of bishoprics followed and established the progress of the faith. Wherever a community of believers was to be found, there religious buildings arose and a cemetery gathered the dead under the shadow of the cross. Gradually parishes were formed. Ecclesiastical establishments were endowed with land, revenues and prerogatives. The pope was consulted on theological questions;

the bishops met together and corresponded; many widely
separated monasteries recognized a single founder, and in even
more cases followed the same rule; men fired with the ideal of
perfection settled in lands far from their place of birth, and
transformed them by their influence; Greek or German bishops
were appointed to sees in Slav territories; lands and gifts of
money were granted by the West to the monastic establishments
in Palestine. To Jerusalem where our Saviour suffered and died
for the redemption of mankind, to Rome where the apostles
Peter and Paul witnessed to their faith in blood, to Compostela
where a marble sarcophagus, discovered at the end of the ninth
century, had been acknowledged as the tomb of St James, the
pilgrims, at first in small bands, then during the eleventh
century in ever greater companies, came bringing their thirst
for penance, renunciation and sanctification; the high-born and
the lowly rubbed shoulders; before the gates of the holy city
the Count of Anjou found paupers without the means of paying
the entrance fee; in 1026–7 Richard, the abbot of St Vanne,
drew in his train a crowd of 700; in 1033, if Raoul le Glabre is
to be believed, the crowd was more numerous than ever and
many people wanted to die in our Lord's own land.

The religious phenomenon was not exclusively concerned
with individuals: everywhere it dominated social life. It was
present in politics where plans for hegemony were combined
with missionary projects, and princes sought to base their
authority on ecclesiastical institutions. It tended to cause
changes in manners, in the relations between men and women,
master and servant, warrior and peasant. It brought about the
formation of a social category, the clergy, for which it provided
the law and the justification and which contained a far higher
proportion of the population than it does today. It gave direction to art and to intellectual life: culture had become the
concern of the clergy, had put itself at the disposal of religion;
in its rudiments, it permitted the celebration of the offices, the
reading and preaching of the Gospel, the copying of Gospel
books and psalters; in its speculations, it took up again the

commentaries of the Fathers and the definitions of the Councils, thus advancing the development of theology, the science of divine matters. The chief vocation of architects, sculptors, painters, illuminators and goldsmiths was to raise sacred buildings, to decorate them and provide them with the liturgical objects necessary for worship. We have spoken of the centres of civilization in the Byzantine empire under the Macedonian dynasty and the Germany of the Ottos: the great majority of these centres corresponded to an ecclesiastical metropolis or a monastery.

CENTRIFUGAL TENDENCIES

Nevertheless, the Church—who, in her origins and object, belongs to the other world but is also incorporated in this— takes on an appearance and develops an influence that vary with the civilizations in which she is embodied; the men she unites in brotherhood in the name of Jesus Christ belong to different political, economic, social and cultural systems, which it is her task to transform in conformity with her spirit, not to reduce to uniformity; thus numerous forms of Christian society are possible. At the beginning of the eleventh century the diversity of the Christian world, promoted by the geographical conditions we have seen, is striking.

What common measure could there be between the Greek towns where Muslim merchants met Italian traders and the state imposed a rigidly corporative organization on the crafts, and the vast wooded or rural stretches of Scandinavia? Or between the long tradition of philosophical reflection in the Hellenic east and the rude epic recollections of the northern lands? In the one region Christianity had already been bound up with a long history, had moulded many generations; in the other it appeared as an innovation that might still be compromised by sudden reversions to paganism. The new kingdoms of Scandinavia, Poland and Hungary were fortunate in having an independent political organization, an autonomous ecclesiastical hierarchy and in being able to safeguard their national traditions. On the other hand, the conquest of Bulgaria and the hellenization of its Church provoked a social and spiritual reaction which, turning away from the form of Christian life confused in men's minds with the hated Greek influence, adopted, following the Greek priest Bogomil, the ancient dualist conception of man and the world divided between the principles of Good and of Evil.

Nor did the establishment of an institutional framework lead to the same result in every case. Following the pattern of the independent Roman foundations (*civitates*), dioceses spread thickly across Italy and into the south of France where the system of parishes, though not of uniform pattern, was firmly constituted. But in Germany the bishoprics were few in number and covered vast areas; on the frontiers of Christendom parish boundaries had hardly begun to be defined at the very moment when, in the south, diaconates and archidiaconates were leading to new groupings of parishes. When a state was strong enough to preserve its cohesion, as in Germany or Byzantium, the Church was centralized and preserved its hierarchic structure, keeping its canonical texts up to date; but when political fragmentation occurred the Church was similarly affected, its forces were dispersed. Even liturgy did not everywhere make use of the same gestures, the same ceremonial or the same tongue to express a worship fundamentally identical throughout the Church: Cyril and Methodius, with remarkable psychological foresight, confirmed by the pope but not respected by their successors, had used the Slavonic language of their catechumens in organizing the liturgy for them; in Muslim Spain the Mozarabites remained faithful to their local practices; Rome and Byzantium, especially, employed different usages. Between the Latin West and the Greek East we can still trace a divergence in the rites, if not a rivalry, some aspects of which we have already glimpsed in recalling the coexistence of two empires, the double apostolate of the missionaries, the unequal economic development of the two areas. In truth, there were two Christendoms.

CHAPTER II

WESTERN CHRISTENDOM

Western Christendom found its first expression and its first organization in the Carolingian empire. This empire declined rapidly before disappearing altogether, but the legacy it left behind posed as many problems in the religious field as in the political or social.

THE PRIVATE APPROPRIATION OF CHURCHES AND THE CRISIS IN THE CLERGY

The idea of public authority suffered an eclipse. Power was measured by the number of men that a nobleman counted among his dependants, who swore personal loyalty to him and acknowledged that they held their fiefs from him; and on the other hand it was measured by the extent of lands and of rights of all kinds—economic, financial, military, judicial—that he held. The Church was endowed with impressive estates, her leaders held influential positions in the world: how then should they remain outside the feudal and seigniorial system, whether it meant laymen securing ecclesiastical functions and property, or prelates behaving like temporal princes?

Canonical tradition provided that a bishop should be elected with the consent of his people, his clergy and his metropolitan; before very long the assent of the king was deemed necessary. In the tenth century it was the prince alone who nominated and invested the bishop. He said: "Receive this church", and symbolically bestowed on him the crozier and ring. He treated him as a vassal, exacted a vassal's services from him, especially the military obligations. The nomination of bishops seemed a normal attribute of the royal function: the emperor of Germany chose them all himself; in France, where the central power was weak, the king disposed of a good score of sees and the territorial princes controlled the rest. Similarly, the lords chose the heads of the monastic communities. The simplest method, they often found, was to choose one of their own family as abbot—which frequently meant taking a layman—or even to keep the office for themselves. The lay abbot did not concern himself with pastoral or liturgical duties, which he abandoned to a provost, but he administered the temporalities of his monastery and performed the feudal services. The proprietor was not above disposing of the monastic properties, and diverted them in part to his own uses.

Within the boundaries of the old Carolingian state another institution allowed the nobles to widen their control over church establishments; this was the office of the advocate, or *advocatus ecclesiae*. The kings had granted the privilege of immunity to many churches; this allowed them exemption from paying certain taxes, and more especially the king's officers were forbidden access to their territories; in judicial matters for instance the "immunist" himself judged certain cases and for others—the more important ones—he led his men to the court of the count. It had seemed necessary for a layman to discharge these functions—hence the advocate; and, naturally enough, the use of a part of the church's property was made over to him in payment for his services. But with the decline of the central power the advocate obtained a freer hand and was able to increase the importance of his office: in places he kept to himself the adjudication of all cases, however trivial or important, he kept the land and the revenues which were his payment inside his own family and turned them into a fief for which he did homage to the abbot or bishop; arguing that, as a professional soldier, he had the men of the immune establishment under his protection, he laid claim to statute-labour and dues of all kinds; he even set up sub-advocates, dependent only on

him. Of what value was the freedom of the ecclesiastical establishment that was exploited in this way by its advocates?

Bishoprics and abbeys found themselves controlled by a
handful of powerful men. The parishes were split up among
the owners of lands. The parish church was as much a part of
the great estate as peasant tenures, the ovens or the mills: it
was bequeathed in wills, or handed over in sales or exchanges.
The proprietor chose the incumbent, had him ordained by a
bishop, and left to him out of the revenues, tithes and offerings
whatever part he pleased.

Temporal power and spiritual functions became confused,
the Church an instrument of domination. In these circumstances it is not difficult to imagine what shifts were resorted
to in the recruitment of the clergy. There can be no mistaking
the evidence on the crisis that the priesthood was passing
through. The two evils of simony and clerical incontinence
were constantly denounced. Trafficking in sacred things—called
simony because it was said that Simon Magus had offered to
buy from St Peter the gift of working miracles—comprised the
sale of ordination to the priesthood, of consecration to the
episcopate, of the functions of bishops, abbots and parish
priests, as well as of the administration of the sacraments to
the faithful. Clerical incontinence, in the moral degradation
to which the clergy had sunk, principally took the form of a
dissolute sexual life and the keeping of concubines. Shameful
examples abounded, and the elder Anselm of Lucca, later
Alexander II, asserted that "all the priests and levites have
wives". The virtues necessary to the priestly ministry had fallen
into such oblivion that a few were found to invoke the payment imposed on every vassal who received a fief as a justification for simony; while others felt it to be necessary for a
woman to keep house for a priest, recommending marriage as
a way of regularizing the situation and avoiding debauchery.

But how deep did these disorders go? It is difficult to say.
The preachers and the reformers painted the picture in dark

colours so as to provoke a reaction; the official records reveal rather the abuses than the unimpeachable and the commonplace. This is the stumbling block that the historian of the religious life constantly encounters: his sources provide him with many details of disorders and excesses. He is tempted to read them as signs of the normal, but he needs prudence to avoid facile generalizations, patience to give true proportion to his picture and humility to confess his doubts and ignorance. Partial but detailed studies that have been made lead one to draw the picture of the priesthood in the tenth and eleventh centuries differently according to the time, the place and the category being studied. A bishop or an abbot was not necessarily a bad prelate for having been chosen by a sovereign; the quality of the German episcopate, for example, remained high. Communities of canons and monks where discipline was relaxed did not automatically relapse into immorality. Perhaps, across the whole face of the West, it was only the lower orders of the clergy that stood out in their lack of learning and worth.

RELIGIOUS LIFE

This inadequacy was the more serious and the more deeply felt in that Christians everywhere were stirred by a new movement.

An enhanced perceptiveness made them sensitive to every manifestation of the supernatural. The appearance of comets, the conjunctions of stars, prodigies—all scrupulously noted by the chroniclers—took on the value of portents, messages, warnings by which a world, truer than the real world of men but hidden by it, made its presence felt in daily life. In the decline of real theological culture, religion became a tissue of injunctions and prohibitions, of magical practices and of sometimes heroic efforts to win God, his angels and his saints over to the side of the believer. The faithful surrounded themselves with insurance policies: they submitted to the strict observance of Easter communion, Mass on Sundays and obligatory fasting;

they resorted to the sacramentals, that is to gestures and exercises from which they hoped for grace: the sign of the cross, the use of holy water, saying the angelus and the use of blessings. The cult of relics became the vogue; saints were regarded as specialists in the cure of certain diseases; visits to sanctuaries along the pilgrimage routes became more and more frequent; the calendar grew overloaded with feasts. God was called on to declare his decision, to stoop to the level of men: ordeals were supposed to allow him to promulgate his judgement, to point to the guilty and absolve the innocent.

An atmosphere of expectancy hung over the Christian world; famine, freakish weather, widespread violence—all set people's minds, in their helplessness, on the next world. There was no "millennial dread": no contemporary document shows mankind as paralysed by an obsession with the last day; all the evidence points rather to toil, to building. But sudden outbursts of feverish activity, or ill-defined aspirations came unheralded to agitate this multitude that was growing into a collective personality, assuming the importance of a great historical actor: it is the outstanding characteristic of this epoch that it saw the development of a "Christian people", ready to further great enterprises.

The phrase from Raoul le Glabre about the "white mantle of churches" spreading over the West, without implying a sudden re-start to building after a period of torpor, at least attests the activity and enthusiasm of a population in which rapid demographic growth and spiritual fervour were strengthening one another.

In the Germanic countries the Carolingian tradition was maintained of churches having a double apse and open timber roof, a tradition of bronze and ivory work, of goldsmiths and illuminators. At the same time, unknown masons, itinerant teams perhaps of Lombards, were working out a new art, solid and coherent—Romanesque art—obtained at the cost of hundreds of tentative realizations the greater number of which are completely lost to us, the only vestiges that remain being in

poor, harsh countries, the mountains of Asturia and Catalonia,
where they have never been replaced by more sumptuous building. What they were experimenting with was throwing a vault
across the nave of a church, reinforcing it with transverse
arches, shoring it up with buttresses, balancing it by means of
other vaults over the aisles; they raised cupolas; by using con-
trasts between stone of different colours and by disposing
masonry in ways that had long been applied in the north of
Italy, they found means of relieving the monotony of walls; by
breaking away from geometrical decoration, they even managed
crude attempts at human faces in the round or gave the form
of limbs to reliquaries.

Again, it was popular feeling that supported peaceful institutions. In the *peace of God* which, after the Councils of
Charroux and Le Puy in 985 and 990, consisted in a solemn
undertaking by the nobles to commit no violence against
ecclesiastical persons or property or against the defenceless
common people, and in the *truce of God*, announced in the
second quarter of the eleventh century, which forbade recourse
to arms between Wednesday night and Monday morning and
during Advent or Lent and on certain feast days, we must
recognize more than the Church's desire to protect her clergy
and possessions, more than adroitness in using the power of
the oath to instil, in conformity with her vocation, a little order
and kindliness into the military society whose rites of knightly
initiation she was at the same moment exerting herself to render
holy: peace appears as a providential necessity, a mystical
requirement of whoever would work for the coming of the
kingdom of God, a collective undertaking. To the peace assem-
blies the villagers were summoned. They fought with their
priests in the parish militia formed by the nobles who had
sworn to take drastic action against those who would have
overthrown the pact of peace.

But this ardour was in danger of evading the supervision of
the priests, and even of turning against them if they came to
the point of expressing indignation with its deficiencies and

treacheries. Here and there, small groups of Christians came together, listened to one of their number interpreting the Gospel in an uncompromisingly spiritual sense, rejected the Church's ministry and discovered the explanation of evil in the struggle between two equally powerful divinities, one of which is good and the other bad: conventicles took shape spontaneously, and in order to reply to the questions that were obsessing men's minds they worked out sets of elementary doctrinal points, eventually leaving the Church while believing all the while in good faith that they were rediscovering the purity of the Christian message. These were not the erudite heresies of clerks, but demands of the common people, simple and vehement. A passionate religious sentiment which could be a source of progress, the corner-stone of mighty projects and an earnest of transcendent successes, found here its potential deviation, a danger against which Christendom needed to be on its guard.

THE REVIVAL OF MONASTIC LIFE

Already, within the field of ecclesiastical institutions, the will to improvement had made itself felt. Almost everywhere there were men who were withdrawing into solitude, living as hermits in order to give themselves up to prayer and mortification. But those whose reputation was attracting disciples to them were forced, willy-nilly, to organize small communities where the problem was to reconcile isolation with the elements of discipline.

It was in Italy that the first successful attempts at monasticism were made. In Calabria, in Campagna and in Latium where he founded the famous monastery of Grottaferrata, St Nilus the Younger, instructed by the Greek monks of southern Italy, installed his followers but without ever hiding his preference for solitary refuges, like the one at Serperi, near Gaëta, where the emperor Otto III visited him. St Romuald, who belonged to the family of the Dukes of Ravenna, perfected an original formula by which the novices led a communal life then, when they had proved themselves, were authorized to disperse to huts in the vicinity and come together only for the Sunday offices and the public confession of their faults against the rule: at Fonte Avellana in 992 and at Camaldoli in 1012 he laid the foundations of the future order of the Camaldolese. The Florentine St John Gualbert, dissatisfied with the relaxed discipline of the monastery of San Miniato, was attracted by this experiment but thought it wise at Vallombrosa and in the houses that followed his reforms to modify it by keeping the monks in communal buildings and dispensing them from all manual labour, which was done by lay brothers (*conversi*).

In the first half of the eleventh century, however, these new formulas that arose from the desire to depart as little as possible from the benefits of the eremitical life were overshadowed by the spectacular success that attended the revival of Benedictine monasticism. Certain nobles had understood the urgent need of putting an end to the abuses caused by their disposing personally of monasteries: they had placed a regular abbot at the elbow of the lay abbot, then given the whole responsibility for the abbey to a religious, sometimes even granting the freedom to elect. Hugh Capet in this manner gave up Saint-Germain-des-Prés, Saint-Riquier and Saint-Denis, and the Dukes of Guyenne, the Dukes of Normandy and the Counts of Anjou handed over to several houses that depended on them the task of choosing their heads. Another guarantee that was frequently conceded to monks was the use of a share of their monastery's endowments; following a pattern applied in the ninth century to the property of cathedral churches, where the bishop's portion had been set apart from that of the canons, a *mensa conventualis* (so called because it provided for the table, *mensa*, of the community) was distinguished from the *mensa abbatialis*, or abbot's share. But the chief point was that the monasteries, with the wise and temperate rule of St Benedict once more observed, became again sanctuaries of prayer and culture.

Gerard, Abbot of Brogne, and John of Vandières had

laboured in Lotharingia; St Dunstan, in Anglo-Saxon territory, had brought under one discipline forty or so monasteries and convents in the third quarter of the tenth century; at Bec in Normandy a school of theologians and administrators was being established; at Fleury-sur-Loire, where the body of St Benedict had been transferred, the monk's mission was highly esteemed; the influence of St Victor, at Marseilles, spread out across Catalonia; at Echternach, Reichenau, St Gall, Fulda, Corvey, in the Germany of the Ottos, numbers of grammarians, chroniclers, miniaturists and copyists were kept busy.

But Cluny was more important than any of these. It is obvious that the influence of a reformer is short-lived since it is merely personal, while the radius of action of a single monastery is limited: its independence and prosperity may be endangered by the pretensions of lord or bishop. How to guard against these drawbacks?

Richard of Saint Vanne, a native of Lorraine, made it a habit to assemble the abbots of the houses he had reformed and give them directives. William of Volpiano, who governed Saint-Bénigne at Dijon from 990 to 1031 and whose influence extended from Normandy to Lombardy, was not content with making the strength of his authority felt but obtained exemption from episcopal jurisdiction for the great monasteries of Dijon, Fécamp and Fruttuaria. But the monastery founded in Burgundy by William III (William the Pious), Duke of Aquitaine, in 909, had made certain of every advantage: from the beginning, it had been the property of the apostles Peter and Paul and its abbot was freely elected; then, under the long abbacies of St Odo, St Mayeul and St Odilo, it grouped around it the establishments it had founded, acquired or reformed and assumed the position as head of a regular and disciplined hierarchy; at the end of the tenth century the whole congregation was subject solely to the spiritual jurisdiction of the see of Rome.

The Cluniac order founded a veritable civilization: spreading out from its capital, admirably situated at the heart of the

western world in southern Burgundy, it was able, after gaining
a firm footing in the basins of the Rhône, the Saône and the
upper Loire, to advance on the lands bordering the English
Channel, along the Rhine and the Danube, work its way into
Provence and Italy, cross into Aquitaine and blossom out into
Spain. The abbot, elected by the monks of the parent abbey,
presented the appearance of an absolute ruler; he named the
priors or confirmed the abbots of every dependent monastery;
the novices of the priories made their profession into his hands;
he was the head of thousands of monks. The customs of Cluny,
which only assumed their definitive form in the second half of
the eleventh century, laid special stress, in the Benedictine life,
on liturgical prayer; manual work they left to servants and
intellectual activity was restricted to edifying reading; meals
were substantial, since the monk, in the choir of his church,
had to be capable of long hours of singing the divine Office.
Cluny exalted the religious condition above all others because
its vocation was to celebrate the glory of God; on the banks
of the Grosne, three churches were raised one after the other
in less than two centuries, each vaster and more magnificent
than its predecessor. But although the influence of the order
accelerated the adoption of the truce of God and directed the
attention of the western world towards the Spanish frontier
between Christendom and Islam, a generalized programme of
religious renewal did not enter into its conceptions: it helped
to make the pope's authority respected since it was proud to
admit his jurisdiction alone, but it remained faithful to the
empire and followed sympathetically the ecclesiastical policy
of the German court. It preserved the ideal of the counsellors
of Charlemagne and Louis the Pious; it did not herald a
Gregory VII. It failed to see that a grave problem was arising
between the papacy and the empire.

PAPACY AND EMPIRE

From Carolingian times, the two powers had been closely
linked: the family of Pippin the Short, under its guarantee, had

given to the Holy See a territorial principality in central Italy; the pope crowned the emperor, but his own election was confirmed by the latter. There was not merely an exchange of services. By simplifying the Augustinian vision of the two cities, clerks had assimilated the earthly city with the empire and assigned it the mission of prefiguring the city of God. It followed naturally that the imperial function should be regarded as a religious magistracy, its holder's mission being to guide his people to eternal life. For "political Augustinianism", the spiritual and the political, the supernatural and the temporal were intermingled; Christian society had but one leader who, according to circumstances and personalities, was either the emperor or the pope.

In the chaos of the second half of the ninth century and the first half of the tenth, it is true, these ideas lost something of their efficacy; the empire was in eclipse, and the papacy, in the hands of the great families of Rome, had fallen to scandalous depths. But with the revival of the empire in 962 by the Saxon, Otto I, the Roman and Carolingian tradition was resumed. The emperor undertook to assist the pope and, as the loyal "advocate" of the Church of Rome, to defend its possessions; but he demanded the right to confirm every newly elected prelate and receive from him an oath of loyalty. In practice, the empire was in control of the papacy and was assuming responsibility for the direction of Christendom; a more or less equal share in the government of the world was hardly envisaged except by the young Otto III and his friend, Gerbert of Aurillac, who in 999 became pope under the name of Sylvester II; the two men dreamt of a universal empire at the heart of which there would exist autonomous political and religious organizations; they applied their plans to Poland and Hungary but their grandiose and ambitious design did not survive them.

Henry II (1002–24), and, later, the first emperors of the Salian dynasty, exercised a strict control over the Church. In Germany they disposed of all the bishoprics and the principal abbeys; they treated their prelates as officers of state, heaping gifts on them, making over regalian powers to them but counting on their loyalty as their surest support; they not infrequently took thought for the priestly virtues of those they were investing; but Conrad II (1024–39) did not hesitate to practise simony. The sovereign of Germany could not exercise so rigid a surveillance over the Bishop of Rome: the emperors left the rôle of pope-maker to the Counts of Tusculum, up to the time when there were three rivals disputing the Holy See. Then Henry III descended on Italy. This monarch was won over to the idea of a reform in the morals of churchmen: like Henry II, who was later to be venerated by the Church, he presided in person over synods and carefully scrutinized the quality of the bishops he selected; he encouraged the monastic reformers in Lorraine and Burgundy; he believed in his religious vocation. He had the rival popes deposed in 1046, then chose a series of German prelates.

This situation created serious problems. Could it possibly be admitted that a ruler who bore the same title as Charlemagne, but whose effective authority covered a remarkably diminished area, should take over the religious direction of the West? Was the emperor who had used the investiture of bishops and abbots as the most effective instrument of his power capable of attacking the abuses that were ravaging the Church? Was the pope condemned to the rôle of emperor's chaplain? How, if he was subordinate to the Germanic rulers, could he win recognition for his spiritual sovereignty over eastern Christendom, which was coterminous with another empire, that held incomparably greater prestige? The remarkable Bruno, Bishop of Toul, who became Pope Leo IX (1048–54) and who wore an aura of sanctity that none of his predecessors had deserved for two centuries, called councils, travelled, widened the field of recruitment of the college of cardinals, condemned simony and clerical incontinence and reminded men that "no one could arrogate to himself the government of a church if he had not been elected by the clergy and the people". But on three occasions he crossed the Alps to consult Henry III; he avoided protesting against the direct nomination of German prelates by the monarch; having launched on his own account into a war with the Norman adventurers, who were setting themselves up in southern Italy, he was beaten and captured; and he engaged in a controversy with the patriarch of Constantinople that was to end, three months after his death, in a deplorable breach.

CHAPTER III

THE RUPTURE WITH
EASTERN CHRISTENDOM

The two centuries during which Byzantium was governed by
the Macedonian dynasty (867–1057) constitute the apogee of
the Eastern Empire.

Animated by a vigorous offensive spirit, it re-established itself firmly in southern Italy, Crete and Cyprus; it rolled back
the tide of Islam beyond Antioch, the upper Euphrates and
Armenia; it shattered the first Bulgarian empire. The authority
of the state was strengthened and its legislation completed.
The schools, in the front rank of which stood the University
of Constantinople, rediscovered the Greek literary tradition and
the philosophy of Plato and the neo-Platonists. The artists had
learnt how to cover large areas with domes or vaults of brick,
and they excelled in frescoes, miniatures, bronze- and ivory-work
and the weaving of sumptuous silken cloths enriched with gold
and silver thread. All the same, this brilliant activity had something egotistical about it, something turned inward on itself:
Byzantium repeated the *motifs* it had inherited, preferred the
encyclopedia and the stylistic exercise to invention; it did not
enrich itself with new blood; it even allowed Italian traders
to supplant its own in the fruitful commerce with the Muslim
world. To understand the estrangement and the breach between
the Christians of East and West, one must not lose sight of the
striking contrast between the two civilizations nor of the proud
and touchy particularism of the Greeks.

THE GREEK CHURCH

In the Eastern Church the same characteristics are to be found as in the empire. Indeed, how should one not be a reflection of the other, when both were so inextricably linked? Did they not form a single body, the care for which was shared by emperor and patriarch? The Church was inseparable from the empire, but this in turn, by virtue of a tradition going back to Constantine and Theodosius, could only be the champion of the Church. The emperor was a sacred personage, guardian of orthodox faith; he supervised religious practices, modified ecclesiastical boundaries and took the initiative in matters of reform. He invested the patriarch of Constantinople, often after nominating him himself. Was this caesaro-papism, the control of spiritual matters by the man who was also head of the temporal power? Or was it not perhaps more appropriate to speak of a theocracy, a government all the ministers of which were convinced that they were God's representatives, all the manifestations of which were brought under the same subjection to the divine order? The confusion operated to the emperor's benefit, but did not deprive the clergy of their importance, dignity or autonomy.

The Church was governed by her own law, based on the canons of the councils and of the imperial laws. But easily her most active element was represented by the monks, those who were the least involved in the world. It must not be forgotten that Christian monasticism was born in the East, where its two basic tendencies, the eremitical and the cenobitical, the solitary and the communal, were defined. The first found its expression in the *laura*, a collection of cells whose inhabitants met together only on Sundays, presided over by an abbot. In the second, the rules for which had been established by St Basil in the fourth century, the monks were gathered into monasteries, were obliged to obey the superior or *hegumenos*, and their time was divided between saying the offices, manual labour and works of charity. After the iconoclastic crisis, conditions in the

Macedonian age were favourable to a magnificent renaissance in monasticism, centred principally on Constantinople itself and the mountainous regions of Bithynia (Mount Olympus), Cappadocia and Mount Athos. In the volcanic rocks of Cappadocia have been found labyrinths of rooms, corridors and churches, covered with inscriptions and paintings, as well as simple grottoes where the solitaries took up residence. A real monastic republic was organized on Mount Athos: the ascetics, who gradually grouped themselves around a monastery, and the great religious establishments, the first and most important of which was Laura, each year on August 15th named their *hegumenoi* and their representatives to an assembly that was held at Karyes under the presidency of a *potos*, the veritable head of a state that possessed a small fleet for carrying the products of the sacred mountain up to the capital and into the great ports of the empire, and there acquiring the commodities it lacked, such as oil and wine. It was from within this monastic society that most of the prelates were recruited, since the lower orders of the secular clergy, composed of parish priests (*popes*) who had the right to marry provided that they did so before ordination to the major orders (subdiaconate, diaconate, priesthood) were deficient in education and prestige.

The hierarchy was ruled by the patriarch of Constantinople. In the East the Church recognized four patriarchates; but after the Arab conquests, that of Constantinople had profited from the eclipse of the sees of Alexandria, Jerusalem and Antioch, while the evangelization of the southern and eastern Slavs by Greek missionaries and the conquests of the Macedonian emperors had given it the opportunity to send Greek prelates to the Churches of Calabria and the new Christian communities in Bulgaria and Russia. The patriarch was the living symbol of Christ, interpreter of the truth, guardian of tradition, second most important person in the empire, the associate of an emperor whom he had crowned in accordance with the provisions of the government, head of an administration that paralleled that of the civil authority, author of encyclicals published abroad by his chancellery; with all these qualities the patriarch considered himself—bishop as he was of the new Rome in which resided the only imperial power that counted—the equal of the bishop of the old Rome whose primacy in honour was offset by the political decline of his capital. Without going into a juridical definition of the Church's constitution, the Burgundian monk Raoul le Glabre asserted: "Just as Rome holds sway over all the Latins, even so Constantinople is the head not only of all the Greeks but of all other dwellers in the East living beyond the seas."

DIVERGENCIES BETWEEN THE EASTERN AND THE WESTERN CHURCHES

Thus the patriarch was tempted to regard the Church as a federation of patriarchates or, more simply, as the association of a Roman patriarchate and a Byzantine patriarchate. About the year 1024, the patriarch Eustathios, noticing that the universal influence of the pope was recognized everywhere, since the officiating priest pronounced the pope's name during the canon of the Mass, asked for the equivalent favour of being hailed throughout the entire Church with the title "ecumenical patriarch". On receiving the Latin refusal, Eustathios suppressed mention of the pope in the Mass.

The dispute did not concern only matters of precedence and the division of authority in the bosom of the Church. It was poisoned by disciplinary grievances, ritual differences and dogmatic friction. Churchmen in the East waxed indignant over the crudeness of clerical morals in the West; they could not understand a bishop's exercising a temporal authority, being caught up in a social system like feudalism and riding, on occasion, at the head of his warriors. At a deeper level, they judged the use of unleavened bread for the Eucharist, the observance of certain fasts and the celibacy of the priesthood to be unpardonable aberrations; proud of their own liturgy, convinced that their tradition preserved intact the illustrious heritage of the oldest form of Christianity, inclined to give to customs the same importance as to articles of faith, imprisoned in their religious past, they saw in their own usages the expression of their national cause. They clung to them with all the more ardour since, aware of the theological treasures of their own Church, they scorned the barbarity and ignorance of the Latins: Photius, who had broken with Rome in 867, had denounced the doctrine by which the Holy Spirit is held to proceed from the Son as well as from the Father (*ex Patre Filioque procedit*) as a heretical conception of the Trinity.

But these grievances, constantly repeated in times of crisis, were not bound to lead to a violent breach: pilgrim journeys, commercial exchanges and artistic influences kept up contact between East and West; through southern Italy, which depended on the Byzantine empire and patriarchate, Greek monasticism and Greek rites were introduced into the vicinity of Rome; Eastern ascetics were venerated in Normandy, Lorraine and Burgundy; the merchants of Amalfi who had settled at Constantinople founded a Latin monastery on Mount Athos; the better informed chroniclers admitted that Greek theologians and philosophers had shown the way to western doctors. The chances of a reconciliation, however, were dashed by a patriarch's ambition and a legate's abruptness. A political question provided the occasion of the schism.

THE SCHISM OF 1054

The warlike intrigues of the Normans in southern Italy were as much of a threat to the possessions of the Holy See as to those of the eastern empire. The Byzantine governor, Argyros, took it on himself to further a policy of understanding between the emperor Constantine IX Monomachus and Pope Leo IX; it is probable that a political and military alliance would have led to a re-alignment of the relative positions of the two Churches. Against this eventuality the patriarch Michael Cerularius rose up in protest. He was beset by a measureless ambi-

tion: born into a senatorial family, he had thrown himself into
a conspiracy to gain the throne; unmasked and thrown into
prison, he had taken orders and, gaining the favour of the new
emperor, Constantine Monomachus, had himself made patriarch. His popularity furthered his plans, and he was an adroit
manoeuvrer. Instead of openly opposing the emperor's Italian
policy he rekindled the religious quarrel, making use, moreover, of an intermediary. Archbishop Leo of Ochrida, in Bulgaria, a former priest of St Sophia, wrote a letter to the Greek
bishop of Trani, in Apulia, which was designed to be published
in this region where the two rites were in competition; in this
letter Leo sharply criticized the practices that in his view the
Latins would have to modify if they wanted to come to terms
with the Eastern Church: he referred particularly to the use of
unleavened bread, Saturday fasting, the eating of meat from
animals that had been bled to death and the suppression of the
Alleluia during Lent; by contrast, he vaunted Greek practices.
The indictment fell into the hands of the cardinal from Lorraine, Humbert de Moyenmoutier, who had just finished com-
piling a corpus under seventy-four heads to call attention to
the privileges, legislation and teaching of the Roman pontiff.
The pope, drawing his inspiration from Humbert, replied
vigorously, affirming the primacy of Rome and waxing ironic
at the expense of a Church that, after engendering so many
heresies in the past, made bold to give lessons to the Roman
Church which, for its part, had never erred in matters of faith.

Nevertheless, the controversy was in a fair way to dying
down by reason of the Norman attacks that gave even greater
urgency to the understanding that had been called for by
Argyros. Constantine Monomachus spoke only of concord;
Michael Cerularius contented himself with asking for his name
to be inscribed on the diptychs of the Roman Church, promising to have the pope's name restored to the prayers in the
canon of the Greek Mass. Leo IX, reacting as so many of his
successors were later to do, thought the political circumstances propitious for a religious settlement. Counting on the

favourable disposition of the emperor, he sent an embassy under Cardinal Humbert. The legates acted without discretion: they deliberately ignored the patriarch; they sharply refuted the treatise of a monk and insisted on Monomachus making the author apologize formally; finally, taking matters into their own hands, and without even waiting for the appointment of a successor to the dead Leo IX, on July 16th, 1054, they placed on the altar of St Sophia a Bull excommunicating Michael Cerularius and Leo of Ochrida. Whereupon the patriarch fanned the embers of popular fury; he summoned a synod which, in its turn, fulminated the excommunication of the legates, sprung from a "region of darkness" to constitute an offence to the true faithful of the Church of God; in a solemn ceremony the papal Bull was burnt. Cerularius now set about consolidating his victory: a short work *Against the Franks* mingled with the customary reproaches the most scandalous rumours about the lives of the Latin prelates and clergy and about the unseemly attitude of women in their churches; the patriarch rehearsed to his colleague at Antioch the twenty-three errors he imputed to the Western Church; he was careful, however, not to adopt a revolutionary attitude: did he not vouch for the fact that since as far back as the sixth century the pope's name had ceased to be commended in the Eastern Mass? He sought to gain currency for the idea that the separation went back into the mists of time.

One thing is certain: the rupture of 1054 did not possess for its contemporaries the significance that we attach to it. The patriarch Peter of Antioch, while recognizing the backwardness, ignorance and obstinacy of the Latins, preached concord and indulgence towards men who were "brothers". The princesses of Kiev, who were married to the kings of France, Hungary and Norway, did not see that any religious question arose for them; a Slavonic Gospel book, brought with her by Queen Anne, was used in the coronations at Rheims. The breach of 1054 was not the first; Humbert's unfortunate embassy could just as well be seen as an unsuccessful attempt at reunion. For the popes, the idea of an irreparable break was not to be accepted: in so far as Christendom meant the solidarity in Christ of all the baptized, the Greeks could not but be part of it and be deserving of solicitude. Yet, in so far as Christendom was inscribed within a territorial framework and took on the colouring of a particular civilization, the events at Constantinople in July of 1054 lent weight to a *de facto* division between the East and the West—a division that in part governed the unfolding of the events we propose to narrate.

PART II

THE RISE OF ROMAN CHRISTENDOM

While in the East the Church and Christendom were enclosed within their own particularism, the Latin West underwent profound transformations during the second half of the eleventh century. It emerged from the Carolingian mould. The Roman pontiff made an energetic bid for its control—which he obtained; he assumed responsibility for a change in the relations between clergy and laity, between the spiritual and the temporal powers; he did not hesitate to engage in open conflict with the emperor. His work found support in the religious needs of Christian peoples: the desire for purification, a nostalgia for the age of the apostles, the enthusiasm aroused by the service of God enabled him to have at his disposal a clergy more fully aware of its duties, and to interest the multitude of the faithful in a cause like the crusade. A Church united around the Bishop of Rome, attached to her freedom, animated by the desire for perfection, anxious to shape the temporal order to her own preoccupations; a society imbued with the influence of that Church, which offered a real policy, superior to such plans as the princes might cherish. Thus spiritual fellowship was reflected in earthly solidarity and achievements: such was the new Christian order, established as a result of what has been called, after the name of the most illustrious of its artisans, the Gregorian reform; such was the Christendom of the crusade, the pilgrimages and Romanesque art. In the first half of the twelfth century, the cause seemed to be won: a saint, Bernard of Clairvaux, stood at every crossroads in the West.

In this rise of Roman Christendom, what was the relative importance of men and circumstances, by what ideas were the leaders guided, what was the extent of their influence? These are the questions discussed by historians, without arriving at a definite conclusion. In any case, the answers are not simple; care must be taken not to idealize the picture or to overlook the strength of certain outstanding ideas.

This rejuvenation of the Church and the constitution of a new form of Christendom cannot be seen in isolation from the great movement of renewal which at that time was restoring the initiative to the West in face of the Byzantine and Muslim worlds. They have their counterpart in an increase in population, an economic revival, technical advances and military expansion. Borne along by this dynamism, western Christendom, under the leadership of the papacy, considered itself entitled to reduce every other form of Christian society to itself: it continued to hope for the annexation of Greek Christendom; it took root even, far from its customary horizons, in the soil of Syria and there founded a colony.

CHAPTER IV

THE FREEDOM OF THE CHURCH UNDER PAPAL AUTHORITY

The crisis through which the Church was passing and which showed itself in the unworthiness of the clergy had never won the complicity of silence: councils in both France and Germany had condemned moral depravity and the traffic in sacred things, bishops had protested against the spirit of the world; but in the middle of the eleventh century indignation spread to the great mass of Christian people: in Milan the Patarene movement exposed the disgraceful state of the clergy and went to the length of refusing the sacraments administered by these priests.

The amelioration that was obviously necessary was envisaged by many as a moral reform; in this view, the renovation of the clergy could be achieved by the weeding-out of priests who would not mend their ways, by the power of preaching, by the choice of prelates who should be distinguished by the blamelessness of their lives. An ascetic became the outspoken apostle of this campaign for reform and, as has happened many times in the Church's history, he was listened to with such effect that the holy man, who dreamt only of solitude and mortification, found himself loaded with honours and official functions: Peter Damian, who had embraced the kind of monastic life extolled by St Romuald, became Cardinal-Bishop of Ostia in 1057 and, in fifteen years, piled up sermons, treatises, letters and missions in an unremitting effort to recall the evangelical demands to which the clergy had to submit if it was not to be found wanting.

At the same moment, however, another cardinal, who had been trained in a monastery in Lorraine, Humbert of Moyenmoutier, instead of stressing moral reform, was pointing out the necessity of changing the very system under which the Church worked. He pointed out in a treatise of *c.* 1057–8, "Against the Simoniacs" (*Adversus Simoniacos*), that this system made the nomination of prelates the opposite of what was laid down in the rules of canon law: "it is the secular power that is first in election and confirmation; next comes the consent, willing or forced, of clergy and people, and finally, as the end of all, the consent of the metropolitan." And the cardinal, depicting the simoniacs as interested in nothing but material things, saw in them simply heretics who could not validly ordain. The abolition of lay investiture was thus proposed as the effective remedy for the ecclesiastical crisis.

The Lorraine reformers offered a picture of a Christian order of society in which the arrangement of relations between spiritual and temporal powers was quite different from the conception held by the emperors, and which emphasized the eminence of the part played by the papacy.

Bishop Wazo of Liège did not hesitate to remind Henry III that everything that concerned religious matters was the sole concern of the pope and that no man had the right to judge him. Humbert of Moyenmoutier, with the help of homely similes, proclaimed that "the priesthood of the Church is like the soul, the kingdom like the body; they have need one of another. But just as the soul dominates and commands the body, so is the priestly dignity superior to the royal dignity as heaven is to the earth." He concluded that "the priesthood must determine what is to be done . . . that kings must follow the churchmen". But inside the Church what other power than that of the pope was capable of showing the emperor and the princes the paths to follow? In the very middle of the ninth century a collection known as the *False Decretals* or the Decretals of Pseudo-

Isidore had produced texts of great age to prove the rights and powers of the Bishop of Rome; two centuries later Humbert gathered together, at the head of a new canonical collection, the documents defining the supreme authority of Rome; it was not simply in a movement of anger that this same man, when a legate at Constantinople, had published the excommunication of the patriarch who refused to submit without discussion to the authority of the pope.

Mention of the breach of 1054 brings us back to the historical circumstances themselves: a series of events led the supporters of reform to undertake the struggle against lay investiture, to exalt the superiority of the Roman pontiff and to make of these two enterprises the means of promoting the freedom of the Church.

THE STAGES IN THE LIBERATION OF THE CHURCH

The essence of the Gregorian reforms, in fact, was not simply the purifying of the ecclesiastical body of its imperfections, as the need has made itself felt periodically in the history of the Church, but more importantly the freeing of the Church from the institutional system within which it had been evolving for seven centuries, that is, since the conversion of the Roman empire, and of which Charlemagne and then Otto I had effected the latest realizations. The good intentions of the emperor Henry III, the denunciation of the vices that were ravaging the clergy by Leo IX and Victor II had led to an improvement in morals but not of a change in the position of the priesthood in relation to the civil authority.

But now, at this precise moment, it happened that a regent, the Empress Agnes, was governing Germany on behalf of her young son, Henry IV, when a successor to Victor II had to be chosen. The clergy and people of Rome lost no time in proceeding to the election of Frederick of Lorraine; the meaning of this nomination was clear: the new pope, Stephen IX, broke the line of popes chosen by the German court which, this time, could do nothing but give its consent; he came forward, moreover, as the brother of Godfrey, Duke of Lorraine, who, having joined the marquisate of Tuscany by marriage to his own duchy, was fighting the German hegemony in central Italy. The combination of circumstances thus favoured the freedom of the pontifical election and procured a base for the papacy in Italy. Stephen's successor, a Burgundian, Nicholas II, set about consolidating these advantages. A council called at the Lateran promulgated a decree on April 13th, 1059, handing over to the cardinals the election of the Roman pontiff and contented itself with safeguarding in the vaguest of terms "the honour and respect" due to the King of Germany. The same assembly listed the penalties that were to be inflicted on the simoniacs and the "Nicolaitans" (those guilty of clerical incontinence), and it condemned all forms of lay investiture, even if made without payment. A few months later Nicholas II, reversing the policy of Leo IX, received the Norman adventurers, Robert Guiscard and Richard of Capua, as vassals of the Church of Rome and confirmed their conquests in southern Italy. But the emancipation had been too hasty: Alexander II, elected in accordance with the new conditions on October 1st, 1061, found himself at grips with a rival who had been agreed upon both by the Roman nobility and the German government; in order to be recognized, he had to submit to an inquiry and wait for a council, under the Archbishop of Cologne, to anathematize his adversary. He strove to show the solicitude of the Holy See for moral reform but he was incapable of advancing the "freedom of the Church". Perhaps his successor, the archdeacon Hildebrand, elected by acclamation on April 22nd, 1073, thanks to the clergy and the faithful who knew the leading rôle he had played for several years in the affairs of the Roman Church, would have been content with what had been so far achieved if he had not seen how easily the prelates and parish priests, recruited as they were, opposed his decisions, and if he had not possessed a very lofty conception of his power, which he made it his duty to render supreme with an admirable obstinacy and conviction.

Gregory VII—for it was he—had as a matter of fact undertaken to deprive simoniac and incontinent priests of all ecclesiastical functions and even of the right to officiate; he had called on the faithful to collaborate in his work, asking them not to attend ceremonies celebrated by those who flouted the pontifical enactments. And as the bishops were evasive and the parish priests protested against a pope who required "a clergy of angels", Gregory, in the Lenten synod held at Rome in 1075, suspended, dismissed or excommunicated the bishops who had not responded to his summons, formally forbade clergy to receive the investiture of a church from a layman and called on metropolitans not to consecrate any more bishops nominated in this way.

At the same time, the pope had made efforts to organize an expedition in aid of the Byzantine empire, hard pressed in Asia Minor by the Seljuk Turks who had inflicted a crushing defeat on it at Manzikert in 1071. The pope was unheeded by the princes and was obliged to abandon his project. Whether in the attribution of ecclesiastical functions or in a cause of importance to the general body of Christians, in his plans for Church government he encountered the opposition of the civil powers. They would have to be brought into line: in February 1075, he combined with the condemnation of lay investiture a warning to the King of France who had conspired in the robbing of Italian traders, the excommunication of Robert Guiscard and a summons to the King of Germany's advisers to explain themselves over the trafficking in churches.

He used striking terms to justify the steps he had taken and his severity: it was incumbent on him, he proclaimed, "to save the flock of the Lord from perdition; he who wishes to carry out God's orders cannot treat ours with contempt"; and by way of explaining his zeal for the eastern Christians he wrote: "what, above all things, urges me on is that the Church of Constantinople, separated from us on the subject of the Holy Spirit, hopes for the peace of the Apostolic See, that the Armenians are almost all straying from the Catholic faith and that nearly all the Christians of the East are waiting for the faith of the apostle Peter to decide between the various opinions".

The reform of the Church and the leadership of Christendom found themselves linked to a fresh assertion of pontifical authority.

THE AUTHORITY OF THE PAPACY

In the register of the Roman chancellery for the year 1075 twenty-seven propositions are copied out, the *Dictatus Papae*; it is not known with certainty whether they are a memorandum, the outline of a sermon or the plan for a canonical collection, but there can be no doubt that they lay down the principles on which Gregory VII and his successors took their stand. From the fundamental assertion that "the Roman Church was founded by the Lord alone" are logically derived the definition of pontifical power, the conception of the Church and the relations between the spiritual power and the temporal authorities.

The pope cannot err in matters of faith (article 22), he gives authority to the canonical texts (17), he is judged by no one (19) but he revises the judgements of whomever he wills (18), he is established in sanctity (23) and who is not in communion with him shall not be regarded as Catholic (26).

The body ecclesiastic is dependent on him alone: he alone is rightly called universal (2), he causes his name to be pronounced in every church (10), he legislates, creates dioceses, transforms institutions (7), he dismisses, absolves and translates bishops (3, 13, 25), he hears the principal legal cases relating to churches; his legate has precedence in synods (4) and no council can be called general without his command (16).

Since his name is unique in the world (11), he occupies the summit of human society: he uses imperial insignia (8), princes kiss his feet (9), he has power to authorize subjects to indict their sovereigns (24), to break oaths of loyalty made to unrighteous men (27), and even to depose emperors (12).

Exegetists have found precedents for all these claims, except the one to depose emperors, but by grouping them together Gregory VII had the merit of defining a system of government such that it assured his control over the Church and legitimized his intervening in worldly affairs.

Gregory VII's desire was to enumerate the juridical reasons for the submission of the Church to his authority; Cardinal Humbert had already drafted a collection of conciliar decisions, patristic texts and letters or decretals of the popes; Cardinals Atto and Deusdedit and Anselm the Younger, Bishop of Lucca, resumed his undertaking and expounded the law of the Church, deriving it from the primacy of Rome. This in turn was openly exercised by legates who summoned synods, published the reforming decrees throughout the West and pronounced sanctions against recalcitrant prelates: some carried out temporary missions, others enjoyed a permanent delegation of powers over an area that was sometimes very wide, like that entrusted to Hugh of Burgundy, Bishop of Die, which covered the greater part of France. The pope did not hesitate to choose bishops himself; he called them together, admonished them where necessary and reserved directly to himself certain questions that he deemed to be within his own competence, such as those concerning the monastic clergy; this method, which had already been applied to the Cluniac Order, in time allowed the papacy to reserve to itself the cognizance of an even greater number of cases and thereby to make its action directly felt in the life of religious society.

The pontiff's responsibility, however, extended far beyond ecclesiastical administration. A whole literature, often inspired by circumstances and marked by a polemical spirit, was written around the weighty problem of the relations between the spiritual and the temporal powers. For Gregory VII there could be no doubt that the second was subject to the supervision of the former; spiritual power in all its fullness had been entrusted to the pope who possessed the faculty of binding and loosing; he was accountable for the salvation of men; he had the right therefore to require that princes, in the government of their kingdoms, should observe the precepts of the Gospels and, in the cases where these laws were not observed, to enact sanctions. He expounded these views at length on two occasions to Hermann, Bishop of Metz. He was not aware of being a revolutionary, nor of making the "absolutely new and unwonted claims for the Apostolic See", with which the French bishop, Bossuet, was six centuries later to charge him; he simply carried to its logical conclusion a doctrine that his predecessors had long since formulated.

It is this vision of the Christian order that must be kept in mind in recalling the struggles of the medieval papacy: lay investiture was the occasion of the conflict and the freedom of the Church was the primary objective. But, at bottom, it was the whole conception, the structure and the efficacy of Christendom that were at stake. This was well appreciated by the imperial publicists when they claimed that Gregory VII had revolted against the order established by God: they for their part drew up plans for a restored Roman empire, reaching as far as Constantinople and Jerusalem, whose head, God's lieutenant, would lord it over the pope, appointed to administer ecclesiastical institutions, and over the princes, placed at the head of kingdoms.

THE INVESTITURE CONFLICT

At the end of 1075, Henry IV installed the deacon Tebaldo as Archbishop of Milan, a position legitimately occupied by Atto in the eyes of the Roman court; on January 24th, 1076, at a synod of German bishops held at Worms, Henry was responsible for the proclamation that "Hildebrand, no pope but a false monk" forfeited his rights, since he had employed fraud and perjury and sown discord in the Church; Gregory VII replied on February 14th, 1076, by deposing the king, releasing his subjects from their oath of loyalty and excommunicating him, "through the power and by the authority" of St Peter: thus began simultaneously the investiture conflict and the struggle between papacy and empire, to make use of the two accepted expressions that denote on the one hand the immediate aspect of the struggle and on the other its wider implications. The vicissitudes of this conflict clearly demonstrate the difficulties awaiting the papacy.

The pope might make it his business to "remove and take away from each man, according to his worth, empires, kingdoms, principalities, duchies, marquisates, earldoms and all the possessions of men", just as he took away "from the depraved and the unworthy patriarchates, primacies, archbishoprics and bishoprics so as to give them to truly religious men"—to use the terms of the sentence of 1080; but he had to reckon with the cunning of the princes, the shifts in power, the complexity of political interests. Abandoned by the German nobles, Henry IV presented himself in the depth of winter, in the garb of a penitent, before the castle of Canossa where Gregory VII was staying; after three days he overcame the pope's severity and was given absolution; Gregory, far from consciously making an arrogant show of superiority or—as some historians have regrettably asserted—committing a political error, played throughout the rôle of the priest who cannot wish the sinner to be damned, but on the contrary is anxious to pardon. Moreover, he made up his mind to recognize as king Rudolph of Swabia, who had been chosen by Henry's enemies, because of "his humility, his submission and his sincerity". But Henry IV crushed Rudolph, prevailed upon some of the prelates to elect another pope, and this interloper he installed in Rome. Gregory VII's only resource was to look for protection to the Norman bands of Robert Guiscard, to bear with the indignation aroused by their ruffianly ways and to die in exile on May 25th, 1085. His successor, Victor III, was no more than a plaything in the hands of the feudal lords of southern Italy. Urban II waited five years before obtaining firm possession of Rome, and ten years before re-occupying the Castle of St Angelo. Paschal II was carried off by Henry V, held prisoner and forced to submit to the emperor's conditions. Gelasius had set out to obtain the support of the King of France when he died at Cluny in 1119.

In the end, the problem of investitures was solved by a compromise, which took into account the wish of the reformers to take the attribution of ecclesiastical functions out of lay hands, and that of the nobles not to lose their supervision over prelates who held considerable possessions as fiefs and exercised rights of a public nature.

Two radical solutions had been considered. In the first, provided that there had been no taint of simony in the nomination and that the priest in question was virtuous, the pope would tolerate investiture by the lay power; Gregory VII himself had countenanced such an accommodation: he had the decree of 1075 published neither in the Anglo-Norman kingdom nor in the Spanish peninsula and he had avoided a collision with the King of France; Urban II had made a reference to a theory of dispensation by which—since the apostles Peter and Paul had submitted to Mosaic rites, although they were condemned, so as to avoid offending opinion—the Roman Church might forgo insisting on certain prohibitions on condition that discipline was not affected. On the other hand, at Sutri in 1111, the delegates of Henry V renounced all intervention in the attribution of bishoprics in return for the promise, which was made by Paschal II's representatives, that the bishops would restore the lands and rights they held from the king and would be satisfied with the goods which were theirs in their own right and the offerings of the faithful. But this complete separation was not practicable.

The way out of the crisis was found by canonists, and particularly Ivo of Chartres, when they demonstrated that the episcopate comprised two completely distinct responsibilities which the Gregorians had failed to dissociate: the exercise of a religious ministry and the administration of temporal possessions and prerogatives. Would it not be appropriate to reserve the handing-over of the one to the ecclesiastical authority, through the crozier and the ring, and of the other to the lord, through the symbol of the sceptre, for example? In 1107 arrangements on this basis were concluded with the English and French monarchies. In 1122, Callistus II invited Henry V to accept them: "Abandon what is not of your administration, in order to be able to administer worthily what belongs to you:" the two declarations known as the Concordat of Worms sanctioned for Germany the division between the attribution of the spiritual function and the enfeoffment of the temporal endowment, together with an oath of loyalty.

THE SCOPE OF THE GREGORIAN REFORM

By basing its pursuit of the Church's freedom on the pre-eminence of the See of Rome, the Gregorian movement achieved results which, though indisputable, were limited and fragile.

It must be remembered that the whole disposition of Christian society had been called in question: the rôle of the layman in the Church, the superiority of the priesthood, the pope's right to lay down lines of conduct for rulers. As it turned out, the dispute, which had at times taken a dramatic turn, led only to a text that dealt with bishops' investitures. And even this text was not very clear. Did the agreement commit only Callistus II and Henry V, or was it valid also for their successors? Was there no danger in allowing the king to be present at elections —"without simony or violence", admittedly—and in case of dispute, to uphold "the wholesomer part" of the electoral college? Would it be possible for the sovereign to withhold possession of the temporalities from a candidate who failed to please him?

As a matter of fact, the princes continued to take a very close interest in the nomination of bishops. They did not lose the habit of recommending candidates to the electors, who tended increasingly to be limited to the canons of a cathedral: by conferring the permission to elect, confirming the new bishop, handing over his temporalities, they were able to keep sees vacant and assure themselves of the eventual occupant's loyalty. These rights were exercised by King Louis VII of France over twenty-six bishoprics, which were called royal; and Henry Plantagenet had similar rights over twenty-seven bishoprics within the great complex of territories he controlled, stretching from the Channel to the Pyrenees. And incidents still took place. Nevertheless, on the whole recruitment to the episcopacy regained its dignity.

The reformers had not overlooked the case of the lesser ecclesiastical dignities: popes in 1080 and 1119, and the general councils of 1123 and 1139 recalled that they did not lie outside the prohibition on lay investiture. But it was not possible to obtain willingly the pure and simple surrender of parish churches or to negotiate with all the landowners who had absorbed them into their estates; in practice, the carrying-out of the prescriptions was left to the good will of possessors. Restitution in some cases, in the guise of works of piety, had already taken place; the movement spread spasmodically; in certain regions it led to the handing-over of parishes and tithes to the bishops and the monasteries; elsewhere, it hardly succeeded in loosening the grip of the nobles. A map of this phenomenon would reveal as many gradations as that of the crisis among the clergy a century earlier. In general, the Church managed to ensure that the landlords, whether of old or recent title, kept only a right of patronage, consisting of the presentation of the incumbent to the religious authority which invested him with his powers. But this change did little to improve the material lot of the country priesthood, whose moral and intellectual condition still left a good deal to be desired. Tithes were still often collected by laymen enfeoffed to petty squires: disputes on this subject continued.

These limited results were nevertheless attributable to the papacy. The Church that had emerged was centralized to the advantage of the papacy, which now exercised an increasingly energetic authority over it and whose plans, in turn, were favoured by its cohesion: through the despatch of temporary legates or commissions of inquiry, the elaboration of ecclesiastical jurisprudence as a consequence of the decretals, the summoning of three ecumenical councils at the Lateran during the twelfth century and the promulgation of their canons, the widening of his jurisdiction, his claim to the exclusive right to canonize, his intervention in the election of bishops, an increase in the system of annual payments (*census*) made to him by the establishments he protected—through all these developments, the Roman pontiff, whose election by the cardinals was now outside the reach of secular interference, had become the undisputed master of a priestly society.

Recognition of this power by the world at large was more difficult to come by. Still, during the second quarter of the twelfth century, under Lothair of Supplinburg and later Conrad III, the empire seemed to accept it. Innocent II commissioned a fresco in which Lothair could be seen kneeling before him; an inscription ran: "The King arrives before the gates and swears first of all to respect the privileges of Rome, then he becomes the pope's man and receives the crown that the pope gives him." The Holy See affected to treat the emperor as a vassal. But such pretensions were in danger of suffering humiliating contradiction: Innocent II, who had not obtained the support of all the cardinals and to whom a rival in the person of Anacletus II presented himself, managed to win the day only with the help of the German army; and scarcely was he rid of his rival when he saw the population of his own capital rise up and organize itself into an autonomous body, a free town, stirred by memories of a glorious past. In the very seat of his power, the pope's security was compromised.

CHAPTER V

RELIGIOUS ASPIRATIONS AND CLERICAL REFORM

If the efforts of the Gregorians, despite the opposition they encountered in the institutional field, brought about a definite improvement in the quality of the clergy, it was because they had the support of the Christian populace. But their aspirations could not be satisfied by an improvement in the relations between clergy and laity; they raised the question of the development of the Christian life and tended towards a profound religious renewal. They found expression in desires that were both simple and deeply felt—penance, poverty, a life of brotherhood. A conscience had been roused in the mass of believers that, when it compared the Gospel precepts with the way of the world, detected inconsistencies and desired a more rigorous observance of divine teaching. These hopes were summed up in the formula, "the return to the apostolic life". At a time when Christians seemed to be yielding to worldly preoccupations, the need for unworldliness and charity found satisfaction in the nostalgic, fervent, simple recollection of the earliest groups of believers.

Social and economic conditions were favourable to these tendencies: by reason of the fact that population was increasing and could no longer subsist solely on the produce of the lands formerly under cultivation, men were readier to listen to appeals to change their manner of life and readier to be led; safer conditions made for an increase in travel and exchange; trade restored the towns and market-places to life, but rapidly accentuated the gap between rich and poor, showing clearly how few were rich enough to afford the scarce, high-priced commodities. Under the pressure of famines and epidemics, frequent in the second half of the eleventh century, the futility of earthly goods was clearly shown. It was in fact in the regions first affected by the demographic and commercial revolution that a hunger for the things of religion was most strongly demonstrated—in the Low Countries, northern France, Lombardy and the cities of the Rhine.

THE STATE OF THE LAITY

It is exceedingly difficult to reconstitute this frame of mind; the evidence we have comes from clerks who alone were able to express themselves; they enlighten us about the transformations of their own particular world and throw light on the innovations that lasted or on those that deviated from the straight line of the faith to end in outrage and repression. They tell us of the reform of chapters and the founding of new Orders, they denounce the heretics—but between these extremes they allow us to guess at the richness and complexity of the state of spiritual ferment of a whole people. There are a few unmistakable signs. Pilgrimages drew crowds in increasing numbers; a whole life grew up along the paths followed by the faithful; the *Guide of the Pilgrim of St James* enables us to form an idea of this life on the routes leading to Compostela. The journey had its compulsory halting-places—at ancient cemeteries, before certain reliquaries, in abbeys and churches —and it had its provision of hospices and inns; it had its legends, renewed at each fresh sanctuary; it had its complement of preachers and minstrels; it had its spirituality, compounded of penitence and joy, of a flight from the world and a yearning for salvation. Thus, whether they were short or long, whether they converged on the focal point of a province's piety or led away to Santiago de Compostela, Rome or Jerusalem, these highroads of the faith canalized the currents of popular piety, stimulated the western world, left in their wake a trail of cleared land, of building and of reviving towns, and left on the map heavier and more important lines than the routes of contemporary merchants.

Of the preachers, we are hardly aware of any save those who were concerned with a major undertaking, or founded new institutions, or incurred the reprobation of the Church. But by themselves, they are enough to give us an idea of the diffusion and repercussions of this apostolate. We may legitimately imagine these men of God, dressed in coarse material, sleeping in woods, huts or barns, famous for their mortifications and the harshness of their harangues, urging penance for the re-mission of sins, exhorting men to "conversion", that is, to a changed life. Men like Robert of Arbrissel and Vitalis of Savigny in western France, Peter the Hermit in the north, specialized in the evangelization of women sinners. Several of these missionaries received licences from Urban II.

If we are to believe Bernold of Constance, writing about 1091, "conversion" affected married folk no less than single men and women. He shows us the monks of Hirschau managing to transform several villages in the Rhineland into fraternal communities: the inhabitants renounced their several posses-sions in favour of the collectivity which they set up, promised obedience to the abbey with whose prayer and merits they wished to associate themselves and, in a special habit, under-took to follow a life of penance. A century later there are traces again of a community of penitents in the marshy plain around Vicenza. These were doubtless phenomena of short duration.

On an even simpler level, since there was as yet no organized form of spiritual life for laymen, individual men or women who, hearing the calls to the "apostolic life", left everything to adopt new forms of religious life.

THE REAWAKENING AMONG THE CLERGY

There is one mistake that must be avoided. We must not be led by the reform into thinking that all was previously corrupt and decadent in the monasteries and the chapters. It would be especially unfair and inaccurate in the case of the Cluniac Order which never throve more vigorously than under its abbot St Hugh the Great, from 1049 to 1109, and which, after a critical period, was energetically taken in hand from 1122 by Peter the Venerable: at the beginning of the twelfth century it numbered 815 houses in France, 105 in Germany, 23 in Spain, 52 in Italy, and 43 in Great Britain. And in the Empire, eastern and southern France, and northern Spain, many were the collegiate or cathedral chapters which respected the discipline defined as far back as 816 by the council of Aix on the lines imposed by the bishop, St Chrodegang, on his clergy of the Church of Metz in the middle of the eighth century. Many of the clergy, however, were looking for "something more": they rejected the material security enjoyed by canons who were in regular receipt of the revenues from their endowments—the *capitular mensa*, the revenue of the chapter as a whole, or their *prebends*, the shares of the income reserved to canons as individuals—and who were thus tempted to abandon the choir and the cloister in favour of a comfortable existence in a private house. They criticized Cluny for the organization of an immense fortune in real estate, the amassing of dues and alms, the constitution of a veritable monastic state, furnished with its government, servants, rights and capital, even if this ponderous temporal structure was designed to facilitate the liturgical vocation of its monks and provide a magnificent setting for the service of God; Peter the Venerable demonstrated clearly, when he was abbot, that a substantial diet and warm clothing were indispensable if the long periods in choir were to be borne, and that the relative absence of manual work was compensated by the length of the offices. Uncompromising spirits could not reconcile this aristocratic monasticism with the precepts of the Gospels.

The first impulse of clerks in love with the idea of absolute poverty was to flee the society of men and live as hermits; but accompanied as they were by a few like-minded spirits, joined by disciples, induced to preach, the solitaries—or at any rate the better amongst them, for we know nothing of the others—soon became heads of communities, and were thus obliged to draw up a scheme of organization.

The hermits of the forest of Craon, on the confines of Normandy and Brittany, are a good illustration of such a development. At the end of the eleventh century the area was peopled with saintly men who cleared a patch of ground around their huts and devoted the time when they were not wielding the hoe or the sickle to prayer and the practice of somewhat unusual types of mortification; a few came to occupy positions of authority: such were Vitalis of Savigny, formerly a canon and chaplain to a noble family; Bernard, who had been in charge of the Benedictine monastery of St Cyprian near Poitiers and who, after defending the interests of his house, had received pontifical authorization to lay down his functions; Robert of Arbrissel, to whom the Bishop of Rennes had looked formerly to reform his clergy. The hermits were accustomed to meet from time to time under Vitalis; Bernard and Robert struck out across the country, preaching and drawing men and women in their wake. In a short while Vitalis was installed at Savigny, Bernard in the forest of Tiron and Robert at Fontevrault.

In some cases the leaders were content to found groups of clerks who dreamed of recovering the austerity and disciplined ways of the clergy of Hippo as they were described in the authentic or reputed texts of St Augustine. Under the authority of "the rule of St Augustine", new chapters of canons were established at St Ruf in Avignon, Arrouaise in northern France, St Victor in Paris, Springiersbach, and above all at Prémontré, where the Bishop of Laon had persuaded St Norbert of Gennep to halt with his disciples. The designation "regular" was given to these chapters, which made themselves responsible for hospices and rural parishes that had been abandoned, or effected the reform of the established chapters.

In other cases new formulas were developed for a monasticism characterized by poverty, penance and manual work. In the

Grande Chartreuse, set in the Alps of Dauphiné, and in Calabria, the Rhenish noble, Bruno, after acceding to high position in the church of Rheims, tried to reconcile the benefits of solitude with the requirements of discipline: in small, detached hermitages the monks recited the Offices, meditated, copied manuscripts, cultivated a patch of garden; their food was brought to them, but they met together for Matins and Vespers, for discussion of the community's affairs and for the main meal on Sunday. In the Limoges region, St Stephen of Muret confined his monks to the precincts of the monastery, forbade them to eat meat or to have any outside possessions. There were many other enterprises worthy of note. They came to life spontaneously from an ascetic's desire for perfection and the enthusiasm of his imitators; later on, their customs were written down—twenty years after St Bruno's death for the Carthusians, half a century after St Stephen's for the Order of Grandmont. The sources of the renewal were to be found between the Pyrenees, the Alps and the Rhine, but their influence spread further afield. There is no better example than that of Cîteaux.

It began with the passionate quest of a Benedictine monk, St Robert of Molesme who, at the end of his life, installed a score of monks in a marshy spot on the banks of the Saône on March 21st, 1098; they had no other programme than to "observe the rule of St Benedict, rejecting all that was contrary to it". The Cistercian made do with a tunic, a greyish cowl of undyed wool and a brown scapular; he slept, fully clothed, on a straw mattress; he lived on bread, fruit and vegetables; he fasted from September 14th until Easter; he bound himself to silence. His day was split up for him by the seven Offices, but was not completely filled by them, since room was left for reading and particularly for manual work; the community accepted neither holdings cultivated by peasants, nor rents, nor tithes; situated as it was, far from normal habitation, it took on itself the task of improving the land it was given. The beginning was hard, and they almost despaired; the odds against maintaining such austerity seemed very long. But in April 1112, a young Burgundian noble by the name of Bernard brought reinforcements to the needy abbey in the shape of thirty companions and his own ardent spirit. The next year, the expansion began: at La Ferté-sur-Grosne, Pontigny, Clairvaux and Morimond were founded the four "daughters" of Cîteaux. They multiplied in their turn; in a quarter of a century the Cistercian plant had taken root in England, Germany, Italy, the Spanish peninsula and Poland, then in Ireland and later in Scandinavia. It is credited with having 525 houses in the twelfth century; Clairvaux, St Bernard's abbey, was the most heavily loaded branch, with 355 houses attached to it.

RELIGIOUS DEVELOPMENTS AMONG WOMEN AND THE ILLITERATE

The reforms corresponded to aspirations that were too widespread to be limited to the more cultivated circles. How should they have left women and the lowly untouched? Literary historians rightly emphasize the more important position occupied by love and women as literary subjects in the twelfth century, and the entry of the countryman into the works of the thirteenth. Simultaneously with her literary dignity, woman's religious vocation was being asserted; and before gaining an entry into the *fabliaux* and the comedies—where in any case he was remorselessly caricatured as repulsive or ludicrous—the unlettered serf was admitted into the bodies that were being granted the Church's official recognition. It is doubtful whether these enrichments of Christian society are normally emphasized enough.

The case of Germany is interesting: about the year 900 there were 70 convents of nuns; about 1100, 150; in the middle of the thirteenth century, more than 500. As a result of some very painstaking research it is possible to establish a comparison between monks and nuns in England; at the end of the eleventh century there were a hundred or so monasteries, and hardly more than a score of convents. In the next 115 years, up to the appearance of the mendicant friars, 357 monasteries were opened, but 118 foundations for cloistered nuns: the men's houses had practically increased fivefold, the women's sevenfold. How did this remarkable increase come about? In the first place, new centres were created in the Benedictine tradition, or in the Augustinian tradition that was based on the advice that the great doctor had given his sister for the group of saintly women that she directed. Later on, some houses sought to imitate the kind of monastic life that had had such success among men: such were the Cistercian nuns who received many novices in the second half of the twelfth century. But the strangest, not to say the most dangerous, undertaking was to combine a community of cloistered nuns with a similar community of monks: this happened at Fontevrault, with the women that Robert of Arbrissel first installed there; they were sworn to the service of God and the men who were subsequently enlisted were given the domestic work to do; after the founder's death it was an abbess who was put in charge of the double establishment. At Prémontré and in other houses that began as eremitic communities or hospices, the rôles were reversed: the group of nuns, whose prioress was subordinate to the abbot, attended to the carding of wool, the weaving of cloth, sewing and washing, while still devoting themselves to the contemplative life. But a formula of this kind required a rigorous discipline and a disposition of buildings that were not always obtained. Criticism arose. In 1141 the chapter at Prémontré ordered the women's communities to be separated; achieving autonomy in this way, they adopted sung offices and, within the Order, a division was made between the sisters of a higher rank who were called canonesses and the ordinary nuns who undertook household duties.

At the same time, many women wished to lead lives of devotion without going so far as to take religious vows. Widows and daughters of nobles and craftsmen, they were alike unable to provide the dowries that many convents demanded and anxious not to part for good with their freedom, but were nevertheless tempted by the idea of turning their difficult and lonely lives into works of salvation; at first they were gathered by priests into religious associations whose orientation and structure gradually took shape: a man from Liège, Lambert le Bègue, who died in 1177, translated the Acts of the Apostles for them and wrote a life of St Agnes for the use of young women. At the very end of the century, at Nivelles and later at Liège, these women, who were called "virgins" or *continentes*, were gathered into communal quarters and soon there appeared, between the Somme and the Rhine, a sprinkling of these "Beguinages", as they were called.

For the uneducated the institution that raised them to the dignity of religious was that of the *conversus* or lay brother. Men of humble condition had for some time been living inside monasteries; but, whether they were *oblati* or *nutriti*, brought up from childhood in the shadow of the cloister, they had remained outside the world, with no chance of finding out if they had a vocation. The lay brother, on the other hand, had of his own free will left his field or workshop, and wished to adopt a new way of life that would gain him salvation. He entered into a special association that was compulsorily linked with a community of canons or monks; he kept his beard, was not tonsured, was not admitted to the choir; he was not subject to the rule, and though neither clerk nor monk his status was that of a religious: he took the vow of obedience, he gave up all material possessions and made an implicit promise of chastity since, if he left the monastery, according to canon law he was unable to contract a valid marriage. He was a member of the spiritual family of the abbey, from which he received not only food and clothing but also the succour of its prayers. It was the happy discovery of Prémontré, Grandmont and Cîteaux to make room for these lowly men and through their work associate them with the organized life of the community. For monks and canons manual work was only a means of spiritual improvement, the essence of their calling lay in liturgical observance; they had no time to carry out all the material tasks of the house. These were seen to by the lay brothers. The Cistercians gave a full and precise definition of their rôle; they supervised their spiritual progress but left them to tend their flocks and to exploit, almost without supervision, their outlying farms. In the twelfth century the institution became popular: Peter the Venerable introduced it to Cluny, where lay brothers replaced the servants.

CHRISTENDOM AND THE REFORMS

There can be no doubt that for Christendom the reforms constituted an asset. The federations of canons and the orders of monks strengthened its cohesion, demonstrated its unity. Its texture was enriched and more closely knit, made up as it was of superimposed networks of pilgrimage routes, ecclesiastical establishments and pontifical institutions. Cîteaux, from this point of view, provided effective support for Cluny. Like the latter, it was free of the private jurisdiction of bishops, centring its influence and its loyalty on the papacy. The cohesion of the Order was assured, not by reason of a monarchical power wielded by the abbot of the parent house, but through the annual meeting of the heads of each house in a general chapter and through a system of reciprocal visitation and correction between monasteries. The "Charter of Charity" was the fine name given to the document governing this regime. On the boundaries of missionary activity, near the Muslim frontier in Portugal as in the Slav territories being colonized by German settlers to the east of the Elbe, Cistercians established themselves and thereby linked these delicate extremities to the body of Roman Christendom.

The religious culture and sensibility of the Christian populace acquired depth and substance through the working of religious aspirations, the endeavours of laymen, the work of nuns and the spiritual progress of the least privileged of the faithful. The task of the clergy had grown harder, for greater demands were being made on them; danger was beginning to manifest itself in revolts against the clergy's tutelage and in the deviations of an ardent but uninformed faith: heresy lay in wait for the intransigent manifestations of popular piety. But then again, what power lay hidden, ready to be called up by those who knew how to detect it! At the end of the eleventh century and the beginning of the twelfth, the most uncompromising sentiment was the religious sentiment, the desire to serve Christ better and to reach heaven. Beyond the divergences of all orders, beyond all particular interests, it was impossible that politics, society and art should not find themselves quickened as a result.

CHAPTER VI

THE CRUSADE

Western Christendom became a community united in action owing to the crusade. The Council of Clermont in 1095 brought out its main characteristics in bold relief. Its head was the pope: the emperor, Henry IV, was defeated; Urban II was sure enough of Italy to undertake a triumphal journey across the Alps; he consecrated churches, distributed indulgences and arbitrated in disputes; he halted at Cluny, where he recalled forcefully that the illustrious abbey was directly dependent on the Holy See; at Clermont he called together the bishops and abbots of France, as he had previously summoned those of the Empire to Piacenza. In the Christian world, the Church commanded respect as an autonomous society, endowed with its own organization and its own laws: the pope took to himself the adjudication of legal cases concerning bishoprics and monasteries; he renewed the prohibition on receiving an ecclesiastical dignity from the hands of a layman; he condemned the nobles who held back tithes; he forbade bishops and clergy to bind themselves by the giving of a vassal's oath. To the Church thus free of bondage fell the mission of seeing that God's laws were observed: it commanded the princes themselves, it ruled society, once the Christian interests were at stake; Philip I of France was excommunicated because he would not part from Bertrada, Simon de Montfort's daughter, who was the lawful wife of the Count of Anjou; the rules of the peace and the truce of God were re-stated and extended to the whole of the West. Then, on November 27th, 1099, Urban II addressed himself to the multitude; he described the afflictions

of the Eastern Christians, the scandal of the Holy Places defiled
by the Infidel; he put forward as an objective the delivery of
Jerusalem, as an emblem the cross, as a reward the remission
of sins; he knew how unruly the warriors were but he trusted
in their chivalry: he mobilized them. And those who heard him
signified their acquiescence by shouting, "God wills it".

THE EARLIEST EXPEDITIONS

Already, before 1099, the western Church had appealed to
the faithful, over the head of the civil powers, in an attempt to
consolidate a Christian order on earth.

Gradually, in the course of the eleventh century, pacific institutions had taken shape and spread. Since their efficacy depended on the mounted warriors, the Church concentrated on
transforming the mentality of this class. It was able to stress
the religious value of the oath of knighthood, which created
moral obligations in whose observance or neglect the Church
had an interest. It introduced its ministers and its spirit into
the initiation ceremonies accompanying the presentation of
arms to the young knight: the sword was blessed and placed
in the hands of the candidate by a priest who exhorted him to
protect the weak and fight the heathen; the ceremony, which
was preferably held at Easter or Whitsuntide, included a vigil
and a Mass. The investiture came to resemble the receiving of
a sacrament: it was the introduction to a new manner of life.
The epic poems—the *chansons de geste*—were to help in form-
ing the pattern of the *preux*, the valiant knight, who was loyal,
brave to the point of temerity, generous to the point of prodi-
gality, passionately attached to good causes, putting his trust
in God, who could not but reward one who served him with
the perfect fidelity of a vassal. The code of chivalry, at the
moment when it was drawn up, represented a force of a social
nature, but also an assurance of salvation: death in a battle
hallowed by the Church opened the gates of heaven. The pope

stated this to the knights who were crossing the Pyrenees to roll back the tide of Islam.

It was at the beginning of the eleventh century that the Christians of Spain had begun to grow restless; to the south of the Cantabrian Mountains they had advanced across the plateau of Old Castile; from the Pyrenean valleys of Navarre and Aragon and the old Carolingian march of Spain, they had tried to debouch on to the valley of the Ebro, which they reached only in its upper part. Small groups of Norman, Burgundian and Gascon knights had straightway been attracted by the prospect of some first-rate fighting, not to mention plundering, and perhaps of holding on to some of the conquered land; attracted, too, through a better acquaintance with Spanish problems resulting from the pilgrimages to Compostela and the setting-up of new Cluniac priories. But in 1063, Pope Alexander II became patron of the enterprise and endowed it with spiritual privileges: he sent his banner to Duke Guy Geoffrey of Aquitaine and promised the remission of their sins to all those who took part in the expedition. Ten years later Gregory VII invited the nobles to combine under Count Ebles II of Roucy. The risks of this "reconquest" do not concern us here; it is sufficient to note its importance for Christendom.

The area of Christendom was increased: in the west of the Spanish peninsula, the lower reaches of the Douro were passed and the mouth of the Tagus reached in 1093; in the centre, Alfonso VI of Castile made himself master of Toledo in 1085; in the east, things went more slowly, Saragossa was not taken until 1118. These victories were the collective achievement of western knighthood; historians are not agreed on the French share in them, which undoubtedly varied from time to time and place to place; but, though Rodrigo Diaz de Vivar—better known as el Cid—may have personified in the eyes of the Muslims themselves the valour of the knights of Castile, it is firmly established that in the hour of peril reinforcements flowed in from Aquitaine and Languedoc, from Champagne and Burgundy, from Normandy and the Ile-de-France: when, in 1087, the fanatical army of the Almoravids, from Africa, had halted Alfonso VI in his tracks, four bands, led by princes as important as the Duke of Burgundy and the Count of Toulouse, hastened down to the peninsula. Intercourse between nations then growing up made it easier to incorporate the Iberian countries with the West: soldiers from far-off lands remained behind when the fighting was over; a younger son of the house of Burgundy, Henry, married a Castilian princess and was made Count of Portugal. The liturgy peculiar to the Christian communities of the region was abolished, and the Roman rite replaced that inherited from Visigothic times, called Mozarabic because it had been preserved by the faithful living under the Muslim yoke. Finally, since the struggle against the enemies of the Cross assumed a general interest and the pope held himself out as the head of Christian society, Gregory VII claimed for the Holy See overriding proprietary rights for all the territories regained from the Infidel.

THE VASSAL PRINCIPALITIES OF THE CHURCH OF ROME

The struggle against Islam allowed the papacy to intervene increasingly in temporal matters and to bring together into a grand Mediterranean policy scattered initiatives that had already enabled it to acquire a set of principalities owing it allegiance as vassals.

The first opportunity came in 1059: Nicholas II was anxious to counteract imperial influence; the Norman leaders, Robert Guiscard and Richard of Capua, wanted to have their conquests in southern Italy recognized: they did homage to the Holy See for the lands they already occupied and for those they were still to acquire, and they promised an annual payment and feudal service. At a stroke, their offensive in Sicily, that was being contained by the Muslims, assumed the character of a religious undertaking, and in thirty years the island came completely under their control. The Norman domination was at first split up into three parts, in Campania, Apulia and

Sicily, which constituted so many fiefs of the Church of Rome; then it was re-grouped in 1128–9 in the hands of Roger II and elevated to a kingdom that was still a vassal.

In 1068, the sovereign of the tiny state of Aragon, which consisted of little more than a few upper Pyrenean valleys, had offered his possessions and any accessions that might accrue to them "to God and St Peter" in return for the payment of an annual tribute. Princes of more distant states had gone through the same motions to extricate themselves from a tricky situation or consolidate their power: the Great Knez of Kiev, exposed to the scheming of a usurper, sent his son to Rome to do homage in 1075; the following year, the Duke of Croatia-Dalmatia did the same in order to be regarded as a king. The pope took the opportunity of strengthening his claims for the observance of his measures of reform. Gregory VII also invoked the existence of special ties, whose weight in law was however by no means clear, in his relations with the kings of Hungary and Denmark. In reality, it was around the western Mediterranean basin that the Holy See encouraged arrangements that gave it grounds for formulating a coordinated policy in the face of the Muslim peril: the pope may have sought to join Aragon to southern Italy, of which he was overlord, by a chain of vassal states; he was able to make dependencies of the County of Provence, the County of Melgueil near Montpellier and the County of Barcelona, before including, in 1144, the infant kingdom of Portugal. It was on a prince of southern France, Raymond IV of Saint-Gilles, Count of Toulouse, that Urban II relied to lead the knights eastward; the pope probably meant to declare lands of the Church of Rome those that were to be liberated by the expedition, and to claim from the princes who were to be set up in them the oath of vassalage.

It will be seen therefore that a whole series of psychological and political precedents paved the way for Urban II's plan: there was nothing extraordinary in his urging Christians to an earthly undertaking, nor in his conferring on it the character of a war against Islam, nor in his assuming the direction of it through the intermediary of a legate, Adhemar of Monteil, Bishop of Puy, nor in his bestowing indulgences on it, nor in his mobilizing the military aristocracy for it. But in opening up the prospect of spiritual salvation, he was answering a yearning so widespread that he could not limit his call to the warrior class, which was obviously the only one capable of assuring temporal victory. A great movement, sustained and diffused by the popular preachers of whom the Picard, Peter the Hermit, has become the symbol, shook the whole of Christendom.

THE FIRST CRUSADE

Penance, redemption, sacrifice, preparation for the last day: these are the needs we have recognized in the religious mentality of the eleventh century, and it is these that the crusade set out to satisfy. It continued the tradition of the pilgrimage undertaken in expiation of sins—a pilgrimage representing a long-established practice but one that had been adapted to circumstances, being made in groups, and even under the protection of armed men, like that of the German bishop Gunther in 1065. It signified a promise of salvation. It supposes an uprooting from the pilgrim's normal environment and suggests an imitation of the sufferings borne by our Lord. There was some idea that it would hasten the return of Christ, who would appear in the Holy City, once it was freed, to wage the great combat against Antichrist and bring time to an end.

While Urban II was travelling about central and southern France organizing the military crusade, hermits and priests and penurious knights, most of them unknown and a few of them somewhat disconcerting figures, were rousing the peoples: thousands of peasants set out, careless whether they would return. Sometimes their passion led them to turn on Jews, sometimes, when they were destitute, they turned to pillage; police action was taken against them; while they were crossing Hungary and Bulgaria the bands joined forces. The Byzantine emperor shunted them into Asia Minor; in the autumn of 1096, less than a year after the Council of Clermont, they were wiped out by the Turks.

This mishap led Urban II to take further safety measures: he declared that the decision to set off was absolutely irrevocable, but he made departure dependent on the consent of the clergy. And as he was dealing with nobles who were possessed of great landed estates and exercised many rights, he placed the goods and the families of the crusaders under the protection of the Church so as to avoid any social upheaval. For all that, even inside the limited prospect of a campaign restricted to knights, the pontifical organization proved inadequate: the pope had intended that the army should set off on August 15th, 1096; the nobles of the West provided four armies which mobilized during late summer and early autumn and did not join up in Constantinople until May, 1097.

In the two years that elapsed between then and the arrival of the crusaders before Jerusalem, it was made abundantly clear that any such collective undertaking of Christendom was bound to produce an inextricable confusion of purposes and interests. No group was homogeneous, they each contained knights, their servants and survivors from the people's crusade; there was no motive common to these various people. Some of the barons found an opportunity to carve out principalities for themselves: Baldwin of Boulogne made an attempt at it, first at Tarsus and then at Edessa, and his Norman rival from Italy, Tancred, did the same at Adana and Alexandretta; Bohemond deployed all his astuteness to install himself at Antioch; Raymond of Saint-Gilles not wanting to be left out made sure of the Tripoli area. There were even some lesser knights who parted company with the main body of the army and fell upon towns. The Genoese, the Pisans and the Venetians, who had carried several bands across the Adriatic, were interested in occupying the Syrian ports and were alive to the commercial possibilities of the expedition.

These disorderly operations did not, however, develop in unexplored territory or at the expense of an absolutely hostile population. Byzantium asserted rights over the whole of this part of the Near East. The Byzantine emperor could not overlook the fact that it was he who had despatched ambassadors to Urban II to obtain help; he looked on the "Latins" as reinforcements who were going to help him to get back the provinces that the Turks had snatched from him; the ideology of the Crusade, the transformation of his request for support into an offensive directed by the pope, was foreign to his intention. He exacted an oath of homage from the principal western chiefs, and a promise to recognize his rights over any reconquered territory. He did recover Nicaea, but when the crusaders had gone on and crossed the Taurus disputes arose. On the other hand, most of the inhabitants of the liberated areas were Christians, it is true, but Christians whose rites, and indeed whose dogmas, were different from those of the Latins: were they to be forced into line, or were their beliefs, their customs and their clergy to be respected? It was the whole problem of the definition and composition of Christendom that was raised.

Along with self-interest and aggressive greed went failures of spirit: some of the barons thought of what they had left behind, and in anxiety or discouragement suddenly returned to their domains. It was this kind of panic that overcame one of the great French feudatories, Eudes of Blois. On the approach to Jerusalem, the army cannot have numbered more than twelve to fifteen thousand fighting men, a tenth of whom were knights, while the fighting force that had set out had been probably ten times the size. Making every allowance for deaths and sickness, the losses due to desertion were still very high.

And yet, these troops could still be moved by mystical impulses. When they had been shut up in Antioch by the Emir of Mosul, a Provençal peasant had revealed to him the spot where was hidden the lance that had pierced our Saviour's side; the relic was discovered and the attackers repulsed. During the siege of Jerusalem, if Albert of Aix can be relied on, the barons made their way in penitential dress to the Mount of Olives, where Peter the Hermit had withdrawn; he told them that the Holy City could belong only to the poor who, in word and deed, were worthy of pleasing God; on the eve of the decisive assault, made on July 14th and 15th, 1099, the crusaders undertook a barefoot procession around the walls.

The most spectacular assertion of Christendom's existence was destined to be simultaneously illuminated by the true spirit of religion and clouded over by scheming and passions typical of human mediocrity. Raymond of Saint-Gilles, whom the pope had singled out to bring the troops of knights into the service of the sacred cause, set off barefoot for the city of David after lingering in the north of Syria; but at the same time he was bribing the more powerful nobles to make sure of their help, and shortly afterwards he decided to delay still further the last lap of the armed pilgrimage in order to obtain for himself a principality beside the sea. After weeping on first beholding Jerusalem and after obtaining assistance from on high by prayer, the crusaders, once they had gained control of the place, gave themselves up to pillage and murder. Did Urban II notice the harm that was being done to his plan, which ran the risk of distortion if the harm grew more widespread? After the premature death, in August, 1098, of his legate, Adhemar of Monteil, his interest in the Holy Land was never again very lively.

One result, nevertheless, showed clearly on the map. The first crusade, brought to a close by the defeat of the Egyptians who had counter-attacked, effected the establishment of Westerners in the East, on the flank of Muslim-held territory. Christendom had toiled in a common effort, the fruit of which it had now to preserve; through freeing the ground where Christ had become incarnate and the Church been born, it had reached self-awareness as a concrete society, having a mission in the world; a strip of land provided it with a reason to make itself manifest in action. In Etienne Gilson's phrase, it now had "its Alsace-Lorraine".

THE EASTERN FRANKISH STATES AND THEIR EFFECT ON CHRISTENDOM

The four principalities that emerged in the first quarter of the twelfth century had every appearance of an extension. of Roman Christendom. Whether in the county of Edessa, the principality of Antioch, the county of Tripoli or the kingdom of Jerusalem, the barons brought the feudal system with them; their lands and rights were held as fiefs; they were bound to one another by the swearing of homage and oaths of loyalty, as in the West. The papacy could have claimed pre-eminent rights over lands won back from the infidel, but seems not to have bothered to do so; it gave free rein to the ambitions of indifferent churchmen, who squabbled over the see of Jerusalem and ended by recognizing the authority of a king. Godfrey of Bouillon, who was the first elected by the crusaders, had only wanted the title "advocate of the Holy Sepulchre", as though he were no more than the defender of an ecclesiastical domain; but his brother and successor, Baldwin, had himself crowned king at Christmas, 1100, in the basilica of Nazareth.

Once they were installed, the crusaders—whom the Arab writers called "Franks", thus unconsciously recognizing the Christian country that had provided the majority of them—concerned themselves with setting up an ecclesiastical hierarchy on Latin lines; they centred it on the patriarchates of Jerusalem and Antioch. In the former area, since the Greek religious organization had been demolished, the task was comparatively easy: metropolitans and bishops gravitated around the patriarch; the establishments that had formerly lived on the generosity of pilgrims were richly endowed, and new monasteries were founded that were not long in becoming the kingdom's biggest landowners. But around Antioch, Byzantine domination had not long disappeared, and the Greek clergy had stayed on; here, the introduction of Latin priests aroused all kinds of bad feeling and difficulties.

It was more than enough to embitter the Byzantines. The

emperor persisted in stubbornly asserting his superior authority
over Antioch, which had been seized by Bohemond and
Tancred, both members of the Guiscard family that, in southern
Italy and in the Balkans, had shown itself the implacable
enemy of the eastern Empire. There followed a period of more
than forty years of complex and deplorable incidents: Bohemond sought to mount an attack against Byzantium; throughout the West he kept up an active campaign of distrust; his
nephew Tancred, after a crushing defeat as a result of which
he was forced to agree to a submission of Draconian severity,
immediately ignored his promises. The emperor, John Com-
nenus, laid siege to Antioch, but in 1137 a popular rising pre-
vented him from occupying the citadel; at length, under the
imminent threat of the Arabs, the prince of Antioch, Raymond
of Poitiers, made due apology in 1144 and recognized the
suzerainty of Byzantium.

The barons of "the Latin East" were thus taken up with
their disputes. But for all that, their position was a precarious
one; except in the north where, beyond the mountains of
Cilicia, the county of Edessa ran as far as the upper Euphrates,
and in the extreme south, where the kingdom of Jerusalem
was protected by the Transjordanian desert, they held only a
narrow coastal strip exposed to formidable pressure from
Islam, which was still present in Aleppo and Damascus. If
they maintained themselves as long as they did it was thanks
to the ceaseless flow of reinforcements and the devotion of the
military orders.

The crusade became an institution. The older historians
busied themselves with appending numbers to them, but they
only distinguished the more important expeditions. In reality,
an unending influx of Westerners arrived in Syria. Most of the
newcomers did not stay; they performed their devotions,
allowed themselves to be conscripted by the local princes, ever
on the alert, then they departed. This armed pilgrimage became
a part of the habits of knightly society, a common religious
practice and a gesture of magnanimity. Confessors ordered it

as a penance. In certain families, from generation to generation, taking the cross became a point of honour. The spirit of mysticism departed, the heroic character was dimmed. Offerings to the religious establishments of Syria became a substitute for personal participation. Judicial guarantees succeeded the spiritual adventure: whoever pronounced the crusader's vow found himself placed under the jurisdiction of the ecclesiastical courts, had special facilities in raising loans and enjoyed a moratorium on the payment of debts. Nevertheless, the movement did not lose all its nobility or all its efficacy; the sincere pilgrims were certainly more numerous than the profiteers and rogues; it was truly a service in the cause of honour that put the aristocracy of the West at the disposal of the Frankish principalities and cost it a great deal in money and in blood.

At the same time, in the Holy Land itself, armed bodies were constituted, pledged equally to prayer, charity and warfare. The Hospital of St John opened its doors to sick and needy pilgrims; its members collected money, opened places of shelter along the pilgrimage routes and saw to the safety of the pilgrims; in about 1113, under the influence of Gerard of Le Puy, the Hospitallers were turned into a military order. In 1118, a few "poor knights of Christ", under the leadership of Hugh of Payens, pronounced the monastic vows of poverty, chastity and obedience; the King of Jerusalem gave them permission to establish themselves near the site of the Temple; Hugh came to Europe in search of recruits and won approval for his foundation at the Council of Troyes in 1128; the customs and objects of the Templars were laid down in a rule: divided into Knights (nobles) and Sergeants (commoners) they were soldiers and also religious, but with a special body of chaplains to keep them constantly in mind of the fact that it was God's battle they waged. The Hospitallers with their white cross, the Templars with their red cross, and soon the Teutonic Knights with their black cross, along the roads of Syria, above the passes and along the borders of the Frankish-held territories built the impressive fortresses of Margat, Krak des Chevaliers, Tortosa and

Château-Pèlerin, whose ruins still fill the visitor with awe. Their commanderies in Europe administered extensive properties and recruited novices. This outstandingly was the army of Christendom.

PARADOXES

The crusade is western Christendom's most original mark in the Middle Ages. It bears witness to the effort it made to subordinate a society's every activity to a religious project determined by the Church. But by forcing its way into temporal affairs it produced paradoxes.

The Church made itself a warring Church; after admitting the resort to arms so as to safeguard the peace, the Church provoked it in order to increase the area within which Christian society flourished. It made of the holy war a privileged means of intervening in the course of world affairs. Charlemagne's conquests had been conceived as religious enterprises, but he had been a temporal sovereign. Now it was the voice of the Vicar of Christ urging men on to military operations and promising special graces to those who should undertake them, just as Mohammed had done. War appeared to Christians to be a legitimate way of hastening the coming of the kingdom of God. He who fought in Spain, no less than he who fought in Palestine, enjoyed remission of his sins, and the expedition of 1145–6 known as the second crusade took on the appearance of a general offensive by Christendom against the Muslims of Syria and Spain and against the heathen Slavs. The hour was not far distant when the Church would use the crusade as a means of safeguarding its temporal interests when they were threatened.

But what is the true picture of those states in the Holy Land, which were held out as the common property that had to be maintained and protected? The families of knights that took root there fell under the charm of oriental life, with its love of comfort, of rich materials, of women attendants, of a culture more curious and more eclectic than any they had known. The

town-dwellers, who were often dissident or heretical Christians
who had deemed conversion the profitable course, grew rich
in trade. Everywhere, Italians were installed; they had set up
warehouses and obtained special districts as concessions where
authority was in the hands of consuls who governed them
according to the laws of their native city; it was their boats
that brought in pilgrims, weapons and supplies, returning with
silks and spices and the rare objects brought in to them by
Muslim traders. A great trading centre came into being, and
the contact between Islam and Christendom was characterized
by joint trade interests at least as much as by the frictions of
war and the confrontation of two religions. The merchant took
over from the knight, and business prosperity, no less than the
honour of the faith, justified the defence of the Christian
positions.

Finally, far from bringing the Greeks and Latins closer together, the crusades widened the gulf. In the thinking of the
popes, Christendom corresponded to the society of all the
faithful; Gregory VII, who wanted to come to the help of the
eastern Emperor, looked on it as a duty of brotherly solicitude;
the breach of 1054, only the last in a long series of disagree-
ments, was regarded as a passing incident. The profound differences that distinguished the eastern from the western community
were not estimated at their true value and the Sovereign Pontiff expected that a gesture of submission to his authority would
immediately restore unity. Instead, the crusades added one
more to the causes of division and, setting Greeks and Latins
face to face, compromised still further the chances of reunion.
The *Alexiad*, the epic composed by the Byzantine princess,
Anna Commena, to the glory of her father, Alexius I, shows
clearly the distrust, indignation and repulsion felt by Greek
opinion: what else than a scandalous travesty of a pilgrimage
was the invasion of the first throngs of penitents; what excellent
pretexts for plunder and conquest for the brutal and rapacious
barons; what an opportunity for gaining a foothold for those
Normans from Italy who were always eager to oust the citizens

of the Empire! Accentuated by blunders on both sides, the misunderstanding became manifestly complete. The attempt to enlarge the map of Christendom contributed more than anything else towards reducing to the West alone the Christendom guided by a pope who yet never ceased to proclaim his responsibility for the whole flock.

CHAPTER VII

ROMANESQUE
CIVILIZATION

Between the middle of the eleventh century and the mid-point of the twelfth, Christianity showed a truly astonishing vitality: not content with establishing a new social order, promoting the reform of the clergy and blossoming out in great popular movements, it brought about a renewal of culture and art by enriching itself with the assumption of alien traditions and establishing new methods as a result of bold experimentation.

THE CULTURAL RENAISSANCE

Since knowledge was the concern of the clergy, schools had grown up alongside ecclesiastical establishments: especially, in the tenth century, within the boundaries of the empire, close to the Rhine, in the vicinity of monasteries; then in the eleventh century around the cathedrals, under the encouragement of bishops and chapters, in Italy and France. Some monasteries maintained a great tradition: Monte Cassino, whose library was reconstituted by its abbot Didier, after being exposed to damage from Saracen forays by reason of its geographical position, now profited from it to open its doors to Greek and Muslim influences; at Fonte-Avellana in Umbria, Guido of Arezzo developed the theory of staff-notation; other notable centres of learning were St Martial at Limoges, Fleury-sur-Loire, Bec in Normandy (where Lanfranc educated the clergy that William the Conqueror placed at the head of the English

Church, and where Ivo of Chartres and Anselm of Canterbury were formed), St Gall in Switzerland, Tegernsee, Reichenau and Ratisbon in Swabia and Bavaria. But in the towns, to which people and trade were returning, the secular schools were competing with those run by the monks—in such places as Milan, Bologna, Pavia, Parma, Ravenna, Tours, Angers, Le Mans, Chartres, Paris and Laon. Through teachers and pupils, moving from centre to centre, influences spread and completed one another.

The first of the "liberal arts", grammar, was little more than the mechanical repetition of rules, for which the writers of ancient Rome supplied the examples. Then it was realized that these formal exercises would be more fruitful if they were undertaken with the aim of better understanding the ancient authors. Whereupon sympathy and admiration began to go out to Virgil, Horace, Lucan, Ovid, Cicero and Seneca. So sensitively, in some cases, was the poetry appreciated, so faithful the adaptation to themes and rhythms, that for a long time classical authorship was attributed to a certain poem by Hildebert of Lavardin, who died in 1134 Archbishop of Tours.

The rebirth of Latin studies opened up new perspectives and permitted the genius of antiquity to be appreciated. Why not seek in the experience of the ancient philosophers the analysis of ethical problems, and then endeavour to formulate the niceties of psychological argument? How could men read Justinian's *Digest* of jurists' opinions, without going back to the Roman laws themselves and undertaking the criticism of their provisions? The writers of antiquity were hailed as valiant pioneers who, bereft of all but purely human powers, had half perceived beauty, justice and truth before Christian revelation came to tear away the veil from men's eyes. It was the intellectual and moral heritage of antiquity that was being assumed by Christianity, confident that no human value was alien to it, when Bernard of Chartres, who died in 1130, wrote: "We are like dwarfs sitting on the shoulders of giants. Thus we see more things than the ancients, and more distantly, not by the keenness of our sight or by the elevation of our stature, but because they lift us up and raise us by all their gigantic height."

This Christian humanism would perhaps have produced only moralists and poets had it not been completed by an initiation into science. In the East, in Sicily, above all in Spain, the Christian and Muslim worlds interpenetrated; and the latter, by its own efforts or by the familiarity it had maintained with the works of Greek or Hellenistic science, was indisputably superior to the former in mathematics, astronomy, physics and geography. A few Christians had recognized this as early as the tenth century; among their number was the monk Gerbert who, before mounting the throne of St Peter under the name of Sylvester II, had learnt in the Spanish town of Vich to handle the astrolabe and the so-called Arabic numerals; and it was not through chance that the best school of medicine was situated at Salerno, until another school of medical studies, in the twelfth century, added lustre to the town of Montpellier. About 1130 a veritable workshop of translators was in action at Toledo, and it is one more proof of the intermingling of men and ideas within Christendom that the best known of these translators of Arabic works—whether in the original or already existing in a Greek version—were the English scholar-priests Adelard of Bath and Robert of Chester.

THE RENEWAL OF INTELLECTUAL METHODS

To make use of these riches a change of methods was needed. But before considering these one point must be stressed: it was not a matter of keeping within a purely human framework of knowledge, whatever its extent and value in the eyes of its discoverers—it was not a matter of going over these discoveries at ever deeper levels, of comparing them and little by little creating one's own intellectual universe; no one would have admitted that thought could develop without reference to God. Faith brought man truth: reason's only remaining task was to give precision to the basic facts of revelation and confirm them

—thus founding on the one hand rational theology and on the other philosophy. Anselm, born in the Val d'Aosta, spending years in the monastery of Bec in Normandy before ending his days in 1109 as Archbishop of Canterbury, summed up this attitude in two striking phrases: "I believe in order to comprehend", for "faith seeks the understanding" of its mysteries. As an attitude this is imbued with divine love, but revolutionary in comparison with that of an ascetic like Peter Damian who only a few years earlier was asserting that God could bring it about that an event should not have taken place.

Since collaboration was possible between faith and reason, dialectics, instead of being practised as an exercise in mental gymnastics, was now to furnish the means of organizing speculative thought. This was the work of two generations. Anselm of Laon († 1117) developed the commentary—the gloss—suggested by the *reading* of holy Writ; he broke away from literal interpretation, and as soon as an important point arose he grouped all the information given on it in Scripture and the Fathers into a *sentence*. Such a collection, however, revealed inconsistencies between the "authorities": *questions* arose that called for solution. Abelard († 1142) quoted 158 of them in his *Sic et Non* ("Yes and No") about 1136, and by means of acute *discussions* he propounded solutions to them. Scholasticism was born. As early as 1152 a Paris teacher, Peter Lombard, collected into four volumes the "sentences" that had to be thrashed out by the Christian thinker; this collection became accepted as the basic manual of theological teaching and for centuries its author was called the *magister sententiarum,* "master of sentences".

The procedure of the jurists was exactly similar: in the first twenty years of the twelfth century, at Bologna, Irnerius glossed the *Corpus Iuris Civilis*, compared parallel passages, reduced contradictions and trained a galaxy of commentators. About 1140 the monk, Gratian of Bologna, applying himself, in the footsteps of countless predecessors, to the collection of the legislative texts of the Church, set about their classification and interpretation with the object of arriving at an "agreement of conflicting canons" (*concordia discordantium canonum*), as he called his famous *Decretum*, which became henceforth the fundamental collection of canon law.

With their augmented stock of knowledge, their skill in psychological inquiry, their eagerness to know the opinions of those who had gone before, their mastery of reasoning skills, the intellectuals of the twelfth cenury managed to give a new impetus to western culture. But they clothed it in a fervent Christianity. Peter Abelard—the dazzling virtuoso of debate, who wandered from town to town in search of opponents worthy of him, as famous as he was widely censured, suffering the torment of his love for Héloïse, mutilated in body—Peter Abelard could recount his spiritual adventure in his *Historia Calamitatum* ("Story of my Calamities"), and at the same time proclaim that general ideas, far from corresponding to true realities, were merely so many words. Like Anselm of Canterbury who, after demonstrating the existence of the Trinity solely by means of dialectics, took refuge in the loving contemplation of God, Abelard counteracted his ambitious questings by an act of faith, writing: "I renounce the title of philosopher if I must thereby be at variance with St Paul. I do not wish to be an Aristotle if that means being separated from Christ."

The dialectical and the mystical were reconciled in the persons of the Canons Regular of St Victor, established in Paris at the beginning of the century by William of Champeaux. Here, a Saxon, known as Hugh of St Victor, wrote short didactic works "on the manner of praying" and "on the manner of meditating"; he described nature as a book of divers lessons that man, by use of the senses and the intelligence, was capable of deciphering so as to progress, through the medium of the symbol, from the sensible to the spiritual. Here too, the Scotsman Richard enumerated the steps in the ascent of the soul, and hinted at the rapture that awaited it at the sixth stage, carrying through an analysis of the love dispensed by the Trinity.

THE ROMANESQUE STYLE

Improvement of methods, audacity in experiment, aptitude for synthesis—these qualities showed even more clearly in the artists than in the scholars, since they expressed in a style of remarkable richness and coherence the unity of Roman Christendom. In so far as there has ever been a "Western Art", Romanesque corresponds to the term. The apse of Winchester Cathedral is a copy of Jumièges; the west front of the cathedral at Bari recalls that of St Etienne at Caen; the plan of Santiago de Compostela coincides with that of St Sernin at Toulouse; Lund carries over into Scania the architecture of Lorraine and the Rhine; the capitals of Nazareth show the same themes as those of Autun; Catalan paintings give evidence of the same techniques as those of Burgundy; Suger summoned goldsmiths from Lorraine to St Denis; from the workshops of Limoges came the reliquaries for the whole of France. Master craftsmen and teams of workmen, no less than techniques and themes, circulated from one end of Christendom to the other.

It was in the closing decades of the eleventh century and at the beginning of the twelfth that the metamorphosis occurred, during the age precisely of Gregory VII and Anselm of Canterbury, of hermits and crusaders, the age of popular unrest and struggles against the hold of feudalism.

The elements were already in existence. Justice has nowadays been done to pre-Romanesque art, which should not be underestimated because of the few remains that have come to light; it had been both conservative and experimental. It had known the complicated and abstract genius of the Celtic world, with its love of interlacing work; had known too the visionary power of Mozarabic art—possibly nurtured on legends that had crossed the Muslim world—as well as the classical regularity of Greco-Roman monuments, the luxuriance of Byzantine paintings and mosaics, the grotesque bestiary of Asiatic civilizations. Nevertheless, these influences, for all that they had touched the West, and were still present, were isolated, dispersed, often expressed clumsily and within too narrow a framework. So technical advances were necessary, at the appropriate moment, for these inspirations to be fully exploited. Over long years, working in obscurity, stonecutters, masons, sculptors, decorators bent to the task.

And suddenly, the unity of themes and techniques is effected. Isolated successes become generally known and are copied, while others occur simultaneously. Every region—practically—formulates its own identity, while respecting a general canon. The essence of Romanesque is organization. Architecture regains its primacy; by the arrangement of space and the distribution of masses, it combines all the arts and all the themes in a common fidelity to the over-all design. It makes plain its preference for a clear, well-organized plan: a central nave flanked by aisles, a clearly defined transept, an apse with an ambulatory and radiating chapels, or else smaller apses on an axis parallel with that of the main apse. It imposes a strong plastic sense that, from the outside, makes the building a combination of balanced volumes—nothing is more coherent, more powerfully harmonious than the Romanesque church, whose elements dovetail, support one another, arrange themselves into a logical hierarchy as satisfying to the eye as to the mind. It assigns a place and a rôle to decoration, which complies with the unified vision of the master craftsman: painting covers the demi-cupolas of the apses, the sides of the aisles and transepts, but avoids the suggestion of too much depth in the vaulting of the nave so as not to distract the attention and break up the perspective of lines receding to the choir. Sculpture finds its place in the tympana above the porches, in the piers and the capitals; or else, discreetly, it gives life to the outside walls, or perhaps emphasizes the articulations of the front. That is the framework established. But the building is occupied, furnished: we are too prone to think of the arts of the goldsmith, the metal

worker and the illuminator as "minor" arts, their products as
relegated to the sacristy, the treasury and the library, or grati-
fying merely a select circle of connoisseurs. But the shrines
and reliquaries display the holy relics to the piety of the
faithful; the crosses, the ciboria, the croziers are in daily use,
necessary adjuncts of the ceremonies; the dearly bought cloths
of silk and gold are the measure of a church's reputation, and
clothe the officiating clergy. The gorgeously illuminated manuscripts enhance the beauty of lesson and prayer for the monks
and canons. No technique is given autonomy; each contributes
to the general harmony.

This outstandingly successful unity is nevertheless consonant
with an immense variety in execution. Earlier French archaeo-
logists developed the theory of regional schools in Burgundy,
Provence, Auvergne, Poitou and Normandy. But the classification depends on whether it is architectural details or the personalities and resources of founders that are taken into account.
Beginning in 1088 the monks of Cluny built the biggest church
in Christendom before the sixteenth-century basilica of St
Peter's in Rome; it had five naves, two transepts, five towers,
an ambulatory with five radiating chapels, and barrel vaulting
a hundred feet high, standing nearly forty feet above the central
nave. But sturdiness and simplicity in methods of construction
were for a long time adequate to the untutored tastes and
limited resources of the villages, while at the same time a more
ambitious approach was winning the day in really large buildings. The paintings that have been preserved betray at least
three different manners, centred on Poitou and the Loire, Burgundy and Catalonia. Sculpture succeeded, not only as decoration, but also in making perceptible supernatural forces, especially the omnipotence of God, by displaying an extraordinary
scope—whether in the composition of scenes of triumph, like the
apocalyptic coming of Christ at Moissac, in covering the whole
of a front with reliefs as in south-west France, or in discover-
ing, as in Provence, the rhythm and forms of Roman temples
and triumphal arches. Everywhere, beneath the craftsman's

chisel, in rude or perfected forms, the passions of earliest times and the refinements of advanced civilizations were brought back to life in the interplay of lines, the representation of weird animals, of normal or grimacing faces, and of Biblical scenes. The dreams, the obsessions, the fancies, the pastimes of a many-sided humanity were offered in homage to the Christian God, source and end of all that exists, Alpha and Omega.

Although the more sophisticated stonework and the custom of building stout vaults were of use in castles, although the fortunes of the middle classes ran to the erection of stone houses, it was not for the benefit of soldiers or merchants that art blossomed thus. It was essentially a form of service to God. And so that art might play its part in a civilization determined that faith should be its guide, prelates and religious communities commissioned work after work, undertook heavy expenditure, had no hesitation in demolishing buildings that still had useful life in them but seemed out of date and inadequate. They were sometimes backed by popular feeling—it seems likely for instance that many country churches were built as a result of the enthusiastic cooperation of the local inhabitants. At this moment, through the building yards with which it was covered, the Christendom that was emerging was made up of toil and art.

THE AGE OF ST BERNARD

This great age of Christianity, so rich, so turbulent, yet already secretly threatened, found a single man to speak for it. Bernard held no high official post, was neither pope nor prince; he was a monk, abbot of a monastery buried in the woods of southern Champagne; he had entered Cîteaux in 1112 because he had seen in the humble community on the banks of the Saône, forcing itself to follow literally the rule of St Benedict, the haven of peace and poverty that he was looking for, away from the world. On the orders of his superior in 1115, with a few companions, he set up the first huts at Clairvaux, whose name was henceforth to be always coupled with his in gentleness and confidence.

In truth, his holiness was the source of his authority and the sign of his pre-eminence. He earned it by his efforts to realize the ideal that his contemporaries had formed of the monk: subjection of body, emotions and intellect to a harsh discipline, and devotion to the cloister as being the setting above all others conducive to salvation. He thought that Cluny was being false to the monastic vocation, was tolerant of excessive comfort, even luxury, and was encouraging the development of the evil tendencies that might be present in some monks; in this connection he kept up a caustic controversy with Peter the Venerable, in which he did not invariably manage to temper his ardour or hold his indignation in check. In the humility, mortification and charity enforced on him by the Cistercian rule he saw the fundamental conditions of spiritual ascent; he himself described the mystic states through which the soul passes as, detesting its sins and becoming purified, it arrives at the state of ecstasy that is the highest degree of union with God, the immediate knowledge of divine love. This religion of the heart dispenses with speculation: "My most sublime philosophy", he wrote, "is to know Jesus Christ, and him crucified." It is aroused by contemplating for preference two moments in the life of our Saviour, when he humbles himself to become more readily perceptible to man: the Cradle and the Cross; and after conjuring up a picture of the indigence and the sufferings of the Word Incarnate, Bernard could write: "From the cross where you are raised, look on me my Well-Beloved. Draw me utterly to you and say to me: 'I will heal you. I will pardon you.' Meanwhile, in a transport of love and blushing with shame, I embrace you." This devotion to the humanity of Christ was reflected in that to the Blessed Virgin: although St Bernard did not admit for Mary the privilege of the Immaculate Conception, with untiring eloquence he hailed in her the advocate of sinners, the mother of mercy, the dispenser of grace. He directed devotion into new paths: he led it from the trembling adoration of Christ as Master and Judge—still so represented in the sculptures on the tympana of churches—to a loving confidence in the soul's Bridegroom; in homilies that were quickly translated into the several vernaculars of Europe he adumbrated a Marian inspiration which was to have its effect on art and literature. Through him the Christian who sought to show forth his faith in all the activities of earthly life found a method of spirituality open to him that was both sustaining and tender and based on inexhaustible meditation on the Incarnation.

ST BERNARD AS CHAMPION AND EXEMPLAR OF CHRISTENDOM

Answering thus, as he did, the needs of his age, he was consulted by it as a prophet, was able to endow it with new life and felt himself authorized to warn it of possible dangers. This solitary was drawn on to the highroads of Europe, he visited princes and moved crowds; he left nearly 500 letters, as well as 250 sermons and numerous treatises.

He never had any doubt that spiritual responsibility and the temporal supervision of Christendom should fall to the papacy. He illustrated the Gregorian position in this matter by taking up the Gospel image of the two swords and giving it the classic interpretation: "The two swords belong to Peter. One is in his hand, the other at his disposal whenever it is necessary for it to be drawn." And when, in 1145, a Cistercian became pope as Eugenius III Bernard, trembling at the idea that one of his disciples was assuming the supreme responsibility, expounded to him at length in his book *On Consideration* what example the pope should set, how irreproachable should be the government of him whose task it was to be "the model of piety, the champion of truth, the regulator of the clergy, the pastor of peoples, the father of kings".

The reform of the clergy seemed to be permanently necessary, since the greater its numbers the more mixed were the motives of those seeking holy orders. Bernard, as a moralist more alive to defects than qualities, has left an unflattering portrait of the clergy of his day: he emphasized their love of luxury, their ambition and pride, their cupidity, their lasciviousness; he recalled the duties of bishops and proposed to them for imitation the example of the saintly Irish prelate Malachy O'Morgair (O'More) who, after halting at Clairvaux, had died there; Bernard's influence was behind the stricter statutes given to Cluny by Peter the Venerable and the decrees of several synods seeking to improve the morality of the country priesthood. Nevertheless, following the Gregorian tradition, Bernard defended the freedom of the Church, that the rulers were tempted to call in question: over a quarter of a century, whenever he heard of a bishop appointed as a nobleman's nominee, or of a disputed election, he intervened, recalled the provisions of canon law and had the disputes referred to the Holy See for arbitration.

Anything that turned the laity away from charity or the spirit of poverty found his intransigent zeal no less ready; he protested against the ostentatious dress of the nobility and their ladies' coquetry, as well as against the avarice of the peasants. He painted an unflattering picture of the "secular hosts" fighting for gain or glory, and contrasted it with the Order of the Knights of Christ with their armour of faith and mail, practising obedience, accepting discipline, combining meekness with courage. The Templars, who were both monks and soldiers, aroused his enthusiasm; he helped Hugh of Payens to get the order accepted by the Council of Troyes and to give it a rule. It would have been surprising if this man, standing at the meeting point of the preoccupations of his age, had not seen in the crusade one of the great factors making for unity and advance in Christian society. It so happened that in 1144 the furthermost point of Frankish advance in the east, the county of Edessa, was overrun by a Muslim counter-attack. The Armenians called on Eugenius III for help, and he turned to King Louis VII of France; but the barons showed little zeal, while popular preachers were already stirring up the districts along the Rhine in a disquieting manner. The pope thereupon made St Bernard the "mouthpiece of the Church of Rome"; with the Abbot of Clairvaux stumping the length and breadth of France and Germany, preaching, writing, exhorting, mobilizing the monasteries of his Order in this high cause, the crusade —generally known as the second—became a matter of salvation, an organized expedition, a movement of all Christendom. It held out to sinners the providential opportunity to wash away their transgressions, to "lie down in the places where the Lord had lain" and to participate in his redemptive suffering. But it had to be accomplished without political irregularity: when, at Vézelay, on March 31st, 1146, he opened his preaching campaign, Bernard spoke to an assembly of barons summoned by Louis VII; in Germany he was at pains to win the cooperation of the Emperor, Conrad III. Finally, he extended the crusade to every front—the East, Spain, the Elbe: not only was it possible for Christians everywhere to acquire identical merits, but as well, through a complementary mercy, "to the host of heathen nations, even to Israel itself, were offered grace, salvation and the possibility of being received into the bosom of the Church". At once the witness of a warrior society and the sanction of a certain conception of evangelization, the Holy War became the instrument for the spread of the Kingdom of God.

At the same time, St Bernard felt that this Christian commonwealth, which he was striving to purify and render worthy of the tasks marked out for it by Providence, was threatened by dangers that now and again materialized. He mounted guard, he intervened, he condemned; there is a whole defensive aspect to his mighty achievement.

For all that the pope is an indispensable head, the rivalry of two claimants for the supreme power has every appearance of an abomination and a catastrophe. This is what happened in 1130; the king, in his embarrassment, asked Bernard at the Council of Etampes for his opinion; it would be possible to weigh up the legal arguments, but there was one decisive factor:

what were the respective merits of the two men? Bernard came down in favour of Innocent II. Henceforth, he put his energies, his eloquence and his influence at the service of the latter, around whom the West gradually rallied.

A few years later the saint was brought into the arena by inroads made into spiritual unity. The Gregorian reform had been in part provoked, in part supported by the religious aspirations of the masses. In its accomplishment, by strengthening the ecclesiastical structure, it had provided the Church with means of censure such that any aspirations remaining unsatisfied tended the more easily to become heterodox. In northwestern Europe, in Languedoc and Provence attacks on the dogma, the ministry and the moral teaching of the Church had gained many adherents. In 1143 a dignitary in the Cologne area, and later a papal legate dispatched to south-western France in 1145, called for the Abbot of Clairvaux. The latter, who recommended force for the reduction of attacks from without, employed persuasion in bringing back straying souls to the fold; he accepted debate, and when his adversaries evaded him he patiently took up their ideas so as to refute them. It was a long-term undertaking, Bernard was needed elsewhere, and his success was not decisive.

Among the theologians and philosophers, the recourse to dialectic and the habit of comparing the sacred texts with the opinions of the Fathers and then propounding conclusions threatened to emancipate reason, and encourage it to construct philosophical systems for which revealed truth would no longer be the starting point. It has been said of Thierry, professor of theology at Chartres in the first half of the twelfth century, that he accepted creation because he was a Christian, but he explained the world without it; and one of his contemporaries, William of Conches, whose orthodoxy was above suspicion, could still write that "the forces of nature should be analysed and explained in themselves", and that it was necessary to try and understand their action, instead of "believing after the manner of peasants, and without seeking reasons". A bishop and a monk drew Bernard's attention to Abelard. The pretext was the examination of some doubtful propositions; but, at bottom, with such an adversary, it was the fundamental intellectual problem of the age that confronted the Abbot of Clairvaux. A private encounter came to nothing; the matter was brought before the Council of Sens at Whitsun 1140: Bernard became inflamed, and trumpeted abroad the machinations of "the writhing snake", precursor of Antichrist. The pope ratified the condemnation proposed by the assembly. Abelard took refuge with Peter the Venerable, and died an edifying death.

Universal man that he was, Bernard did not omit to assign to art its meaning and its limitations. Mere prettiness, when its destination was a monastic building, he found reprehensible: he waxed indignant over the decoration of the abbey church of Cluny. For his Order he desired unadorned churches, without tiled paving, without painting or sculpture save only a crucifix; he wished Cistercian craftsmen not to illuminate manuscripts; bare walls and plain letters, witnesses to the spirit of poverty, could suffice for the liturgy. On the other hand, it was right that ecclesiastical art should be comprehensible to "the senseless and the ignorant", and should have recourse to "material ornamentation so as to arouse to devotion the people of the carnal sort": just as the Song of Songs held out images of the mystical life to St Bernard, the symbolism found in the house of God should help the simple to glimpse the realities of the heavenly Jerusalem.

Western Christendom has known headier moments, more spectacular intellectual achievements than during the quarter-century (1127–53) that contains the public life of St Bernard, but it is almost certainly under the authority of the Abbot of Clairvaux that it was the most closely knit and the most clearly animated in the name of a purely religious principle; by the same token, it has demonstrated in the clearest fashion its potentialities and its contingency.

CHAPTER VIII

DANGERS IN THE SECOND HALF OF THE TWELFTH CENTURY

In the second half of the twelfth century, dangers took shape that were not all averted, and none of them vanished completely from the scene.

THE GROWTH OF HERESY

The most serious threat sprang from the religious hunger of the masses: in the name of poverty and asceticism, it tended to transfer from the Church to mere laymen, noted for their exemplary life, the right to teach and to absolve; its logical result was the simplification of the sacraments and the suppression of the hierarchy.

Spontaneously, following the call of a hermit or a mere believer, small groups came together in secret in the Low Countries, in the Rhineland, in Champagne, Lombardy and the south of France; they were reinforced by the artisans, who were more sensitive to social inequalities and the injustices of fortune; these heretics were often known as "weavers" (from the part they played in the developing textile industry of Lombardy). A few popular leaders provoked more widespread movements: Peter of Bruys and Henry of Lausanne in Languedoc and Provence, Arnold of Brescia—who was in fact an intellectual—in Lombardy and later at Rome. It appeared that, in order to recover genuine religion, it was enough to read the Bible and apply its lessons: this was the view of a Lyons merchant, Peter Waldo who, about 1176, gave away his belongings, had the text of the Gospels copied and, with a handful of followers, set out on a successful mission through the valleys of the Dauphiné and upper Provence, and later Piedmont. They were simple men, speaking in familiar language, calling on the Holy Spirit for their inspiration so as to be worthy to preside over the Lord's Supper and grant remission of sins.

A few heterodox preachers rejected Christian morality. They denied the value of marriage and looked with a tolerant eye on sexual irregularities, on the ground that the disorders of the flesh could not affect the life of the soul. In their case, a dualist conception of the world seems to have provided a very convenient explanation and justification.

About the smaller conventicles, the ecclesiastical authorities had only vague information, and were inclined to regard them as centres of debauchery. The clergy naturally opposed the views ascribed to the heretics with the weapons they were familiar with: nurtured on St Augustine, they thought they were confronted with the Manichean doctrine that the Bishop of Hippo had fought. Modern historians have for a long time been deceived by this identification, and have exercised their imagination in trying to link the heresies of the twelfth century with those of Mani, which had their origin in the third century, in Iran. The western heresies of the twelfth century arose spontaneously, and have scarcely any doctrinal content. But it is true to say, on the other hand, that after 1150, in the south of Europe, they became so consistent and organized that they were transformed into a veritable Church, opposed to the Church of Rome.

In eastern Christendom, since the tenth century, there had been propagated the heresy of the Bulgarian priest Bogomil; on its passage to Constantinople and Asia Minor it had gathered to itself all the residue of heresy contained in a region of long-established spiritual fermentation, particularly the Manichean theses long defended by groups of Paulicians. It had provoked imperial intervention, but it had insinuated itself and then taken root in the mountains of Serbia and Bosnia, on the frontiers of the Latin and Greek spheres of influence; it became the unifying principle of ethnic groups, and in 1199 the Ban of Bosnia became an adherent. Under the guidance of bishops who built churches with frescoes of outstanding beauty, the heretics thought it incumbent on them to spread their beliefs. The increasing frequency of contacts, through crusades and penetration by traders, helped their plans. In Italy and in Languedoc their views found the ground prepared and tapped aspirations no longer satisfied by the Church of Rome; an organizational framework was set up. In this way dioceses were founded in Lombardy, the Marches, Umbria and even up as far as the northern Ecclesiastical States, in Piedmont. A Bogomile bishop from Constantinople, Nicetas, called a "council" at Saint-Félix-de-Caraman, near Toulouse, in 1167 or 1172. In spite of St Bernard's preaching campaign, many of the faithful in Languedoc had forsaken the Church; a first organization, comprising four separate districts, had been adumbrated and was confirmed by Nicetas; at the same time, he gained recognition for the dogma and the ritual that had been adopted in the Balkans.

The heresy of southern France had been established. It had its institutions, in the form of bishops assisted by deacons. It taught that the world is the work of the evil God, Satan or Lucifer; that the soul, created by the righteous God, is imprisoned in the body but that after the coming of Christ, who had no contact with impure matter and whose human form was an appearance only, its delivery was possible. Men had to renounce the works of the flesh, abstain from any food that was the product of procreation, and fast. Those who swore themselves to this harsh rule received a sacrament—the *Consolamentum*—after which they became the "pure", the *Perfect* or *Cathari*; they lived a communal life, bound themselves to poverty and undertook a life of service to those around them. The Perfect who failed in his vocation, and the "Believer" who had not received the *Consolamentum* were destined to undergo as many reincarnations as might be necessary to detach them from the tyranny of matter. This was the only punishment, since there was neither purgatory nor hell; the righteous God would certainly triumph, but no one knew at what moment he would gather all souls to himself.

At the Council of Tours in 1163 the pope had given the name "Albigenses" to the heretics of Languedoc. Their proliferation appeared to disconcert those who were responsible for Christian society; simple and robust, accommodating in practice and exacting in its ideal, the heresy found many sympathizers. The reaction of the clergy was clumsy; sometimes it was left to the mass of the faithful to express indignation, as when they burnt Peter of Bruys, who had attacked the crucifix. Slowly, repressive measures were published: the discovery of the heretics was made the responsibility of the bishops who pronounced spiritual sanctions; these were accompanied by temporal penalties—confiscation of property, deprivation of rights or chastisement—that only the civil power could apply. But there was the case of the Viscount of Béziers, who preferred to protect the heretics; in 1181 a cardinal organized an expedition against him. On what strange roads was the Church hazarding itself to be rid of the worst scourge that attended it?

THE CASE OF THOMAS BECKET

The fierce conflict that set Church and Crown at odds in England provides a good example of the difficulties the religious power was likely to encounter when it busied itself with giving orders to the civil power, in a case where the latter not only refused to acknowledge itself to be of inferior status but even laid claim to a rigorous supervision of ecclesiastical institutions. It was not a matter of confusion between clerical and lay society, as it had been in the tenth century (a confusion which in any case had not been completely cleared up, in view of the Church's wealth and the only partial success of the Gregorian reforms); it was a matter of the conscious claims, based on law, of a power growing in strength, of the monarchy.

Jurists, more often than not sprung from ecclesiastical circles where the study of canon law encouraged speculation, were found to justify the policy of strength adopted by Henry II of England. Richard Fitz Neal, who was both minister and bishop, noted that "the care of their subjects had been vouchsafed to kings by God himself", and that kings were dependent only on the judgement of God. Renouf Glenville revived the maxim from the *Institutes* of Justinian: "that which has pleased the sovereign has the force of law". In practical terms, this amounted to a threat to the famous "freedom of the Church", by reason of which the clergy was a distinct and eminent "order" of society, enjoying, among other privileges, the judicial one of the "forum" or separate tribunal.

Thomas Becket intervened. He had begun his career by serving the authoritarian policy of Henry II, who entrusted him with the chancellorship, and had rewarded him by procuring his election as Archbishop of Canterbury in 1162. But, in this elevated position, subjected to a spiritual evolution that estranged him from luxury and the world, he consecrated to the defence of ecclesiastical prerogatives his inflexible and impassioned character as well as his juridical knowledge. As early as 1163 he refused to pay a tax that he considered to be unwarranted, and to hand over to the king's courts members of the clergy convicted of crimes. The king thought he would vanquish him by proving that his present demands went no further than to reproduce the ancient customs of England, a list of which was drawn up in the Constitutions of Clarendon. Becket lost countenance; the English bishops dared not protest; but on two occasions Alexander III refused to approve the Constitutions: he could not admit that the control of the papacy over the Church and the fate of the clergy should be subordinated to the will of a prince.

The archbishop saw his duty plainly: he accused himself of having betrayed the Church's interests. The crisis came to a head; he was summoned to a council at Nottingham, but fled to France during the night of October 13th–14th, 1164. For six years, between excommunications hurled by the exile at his enemy's counsellors and complaisant prelates on the one hand, and pressure on the other from Henry on the pope and the King of France, the conflict dragged on. Wearying at last of the struggle, Henry agreed to a reconciliation; the archbishop took up possession of his see and immediately set about eliminating the bishops who had failed to support him. Henry, in Normandy at the time, complained of such zeal. Four knights thought to discharge their feudal obligation to espouse their lord's cause by crossing the Channel and murdering Thomas, before the altar of his cathedral, on December 29th, 1170.

The outcry was tremendous. Henry II was obliged to submit to penance before he could obtain reconciliation with the Church, at Avranches on May 21st, 1172. He undertook to abandon the practices that had been introduced during his reign. All the same, within three years he made the papal legate admit that the infringement of certain regulations fell solely within the competence of the royal courts, and he reserved to himself the possibility of requiring from the clergy an oath not to undertake anything against the good of his person or his kingdom. Basically, the monarchy was giving up nothing. But Thomas Becket, who was canonized on March 10th, 1173, and whose tomb became a place of pilgrimage, was proclaimed a martyr for the freedom of the Church and the defender of the Gregorian ideal.

THE PRETENSIONS OF FREDERICK BARBAROSSA

In the policy of Frederick Barbarossa, who was elected King of Germany in 1152, the rôle of the Holy See and the very organization of Christendom were envisaged in a new light. His immediate objective was the restoration to the crown of all the rights which it had let slip from its grasp in Germany and Italy: the Concordat of Worms, which provided for the presence of the sovereign or his representative at the election of bishops,

was interpreted in such a way as to permit the choice of prelates who could be relied on; and in any case, the investing of
new bishops with their temporalities, and the impossibility of
holding any public powers without the authorization of the
monarch offered numerous and easy means of assuring the
docility of the princes of the Church. The public law of ancient
Rome in imperial times, rediscovered by the jurists in the
schools of Bologna, suggested that the power of the sovereign
over his own states was unlimited. To the south as well as to
the north of the Alps, Frederick showed himself intent on en-
forcing his rights.

Moreover, his idea of the empire was a lofty one. He was
convinced that the origin of his power lay in Rome: after the
Babylonians, the Persians and the Greco-Macedonians, the
authority over the world had been entrusted to the Romans, by
whom it had been successively delegated to the Latin princes,
then to the Franks and finally to the Germans. The various
kings governed only "provinces" within the framework of the
empire, whose head, following the example of Charlemagne
who had been crowned and anointed by the Church and who
had supervised the papacy, guided its destiny in the way of
God. How, supported by the Carolingian recollection of a religious monarchy, heir to the universal ambitions of Rome, and
beneficiary of the restoration to honour of the idea of state
sovereignty, should Frederick Barbarossa not have threatened
to subvert the Gregorian conception of the Christian ordering
of society? He was impatient of any manifestation of the latter.
At the Diet of Besançon (1152), he understood the legates to
intimate that he had received from the Roman Church great
"benefices", as though he held his empire as a fief of the
Church: he drove them out and forbade the German bishops to
attend the Curia. On receiving representations in the matter
of papal rights in Rome, he declared that "Emperor of the
Romans by divine ordination, he would have no more than the
shadow of power and an empty title with no real value, if he
was stripped of his authority over the city of the Caesars".

At first, circumstances favoured his plans: the pope did not even feel himself secure in Rome, where he had recognized the communes and where the population had been worked upon by Arnold of Brescia. He had lost the King of Sicily's support. So he was happy for Frederick to come down into Italy and bring Rome to heel—a service for which he crowned him emperor in 1155. Four years later there arose an opportunity to revive the old imperial right to supervise the pontifical election: Adrian IV had died, and the majority voted for Roland Bandinelli who chose the name Alexander III; a minority had Cardinal Octavian acclaimed Victor IV. The emperor summoned the bishops of the West to a council at Pavia to decide between the merits of the two candidates: the universal and religious vocation of the empire was about to be unequivocally demonstrated.

But only Victor IV appeared in Pavia. Alexander III, who had taught canon law and been head of the papal chancellery, was well placed to recall that the Church of Rome alone was empowered to judge ecclesiastical cases and could not itself be judged. The imperial assembly pronounced in favour of Victor IV, but Alexander III excommunicated Frederick and his pope, gained the recognition of France, England, the Spanish kingdoms, Sicily and Norway and, the better to protect himself from the forays of the emperor into Italy, took refuge with Louis VII of France (1161).

The struggle dragged on until 1177. Frederick's advisers, desiring to place their master's cause under the illustrious and significant protection of Charlemagne, pronounced his canonization at Aix-la-Chapelle. But on his side, Alexander III had the towns of Lombardy—who were implacable enemies of the emperor's authoritarian policy—the unwavering support of the French king, and the plague which decimated the German army in the very hour of its triumph. At Venice, Frederick prostrated himself before the legitimate pontiff before receiving from him the kiss of peace. Two years later, Alexander III called a general council at the Lateran (the third Lateran and tenth General Council) which ratified the progress made in Roman centralization.

Yet Frederick's humiliation at Venice had done him no more damage than Henry IV's, exactly a century before, at Canossa. The emperor quickly recovered the ground he had lost; he showed himself firm in Germany and flexible in Italy. He detached the cities of the north from their alliance with the pope; he maintained his positions in Tuscany; he married his son to the heiress to the kingdom of Sicily, so that the patrimony of the Roman Church was threatened with encirclement. Of what weight were the doctrinal assertions of the papacy when temporal circumstances were forcing it into obscurity?

Moreover, a new aura came to surround the empire. Frederick took the cross, but was drowned crossing a small river in Cilicia. The popular imagination seized only on his death in a distant land. Predictions had long been in circulation to the effect that the last emperor would come to Jerusalem and offer to God the world gathered up in his power; then Antichrist would arise, and finally the Lord would gain the victory. Was it not likely that Frederick I, who had vanished on his way to the Holy Land, would reappear in the form of the emperor of the last days?

THE ROYAL CRUSADES

The expeditions to the East were henceforth a matter for the princes. When the Muslim pressure on the Latin states in Syria was increased, it was to them that the religious leaders appealed for substantial reinforcements. If they did not take part, then help would be insignificant, but if they did the Church would lose control of the crusade. There was now no ignoring them, as Urban II had done in his appeal at Clermont; their entry into the war had to be negotiated. When Edessa fell in 1144, Eugenius III and St Bernard solicited the King of France and the emperor. From now on the papacy was reduced to using diplomacy in trying to save what the mystical enthusiasm of western Christians had created on the soil of the East.

The second crusade—that of Louis VII of France and
Conrad III of Germany—was beset by intrigue. Far from
winning help from the Byzantines it fanned their mistrust and
engendered the most serious friction with them. The two kings
were separated and defeated in Asia Minor; instead of relieving
the county of Edessa and the principality of Antioch, they
allowed themselves to be drawn off towards the south by
King Baldwin III of Jerusalem, who launched them on an unsuccessful offensive against Damascus. They came out of it at
variance with the eastern emperor and the Franks of Syria,
whom they accused of treachery.

The Latin princes of the East then drew nearer to the head
of the eastern empire and conceived the idea of attacking Egypt
so as to prevent the descendants of the Turk Zengi from attach-
ing it to their possessions in Syria and thus accomplishing an
encirclement that the small Christian states could not tolerate.
Their efforts failed; Saladin, regrouping the Levantine Muslims
under his authority, crushed the Frankish knights at Hattin and
entered Jerusalem in 1187.

The feelings of the West can be imagined. A major expedition was immediately decided on, but the decision was imple-
mented haltingly. The first to set out was the Emperor
Frederick; after an inept reception from the eastern emperor,
Isaac Angelus, he sacked Adrianople and came within an ace
of ordering his troops to attack Constantinople; he had got no
farther than Cilicia when he was drowned. The King of France,
Philip-Augustus, was wholly occupied in egging on the younger
sons of Henry Plantagenet to rebel against their father, then
with fighting Richard I of England, the new master of the
Anglo-Angevin lands, when he was more or less obliged to
take the cross, along with his rival. There could be no more
than a precarious understanding between the two men. The
cause of the Holy Land had meanwhile attracted contingents
from all sides; Acre was retaken in 1191, but Louis hastened
back to his kingdom; Richard, splendid in his valour but un-
bearably insolent, relieved the coast but was unable to recover

Jerusalem. At least he had made Cyprus available to the western forces, but this noteworthy base of operations, ruled over by the Lusignan family, had been wrested from the Byzantines.

When Henry VI, son and successor to Frederick Barbarossa, took the crusader's vow in 1195, the holy war took on the complexion of an attempt at universal domination. The author of this bid was heir not only to the imperial tradition and the eastern policy of the kings of Sicily, but to the prophecies of the Apocalypse as well; as a result of his visionary ambition he tended to see himself as responsible for a cause that involved the whole of the West and, by reason of this pre-eminent responsibility, to force the pope and the kings of the West to back his plans and recognize his supreme authority. He wanted the pope to make the imperial succession hereditary in the Hohenstaufen family, as the royal succession was in the kingdom of Sicily; he set about making vassal or tributary kingdoms subordinate to the Empire: he had maintained his suzerainty over Poland; he had obliged Richard Cœur-de-Lion, who had fallen into his hands, to acknowledge himself his vassal as regards England; he hoped to obtain the homage of the kings of Castile and Aragon, and probably of the Latin principalities in the East; he had promises in this sense from the kings of Lesser Armenia and Cyprus; he had been responsible for the marriage of his brother Philip to a Greek princess, the daughter of a dethroned emperor; he levied a tribute on the Muslim princes of North Africa.

His lieutenants had landed at Acre; another army was about to set sail for Constantinople; the aged Pope Celestine III had no resource but inertia against projects that were ruining Roman Christendom, when Henry VI was struck down by a fever at Messina on September 28th, 1197.

CHAPTER IX

INNOCENT III

A few months later, on January 8th, 1198, the cardinals elected to the see of Rome their youngest member, Lothair Conti, son of Count Trasimund of Segni. In him were combined the feeling and the taste for action of his ancient and noble Latin family with the culture of a one-time pupil in the schools of Paris and Bologna, a profound piety with knowledge of administration, since his uncle, Clement III, had raised him to the cardinalate in 1190; he was no less capable of profiting from circumstances than of expounding the theory of pontifical power. He did not compose a corpus of doctrine, but affirmed, under the pressure of events, the reasons underlying his policy. Our approach, then, should be to watch him at work and listen to his justification of it.

THE GOVERNMENT OF THE CHURCH

The plenitude of power enjoyed by the pope was exercised uncompromisingly in the administration of the Church. Innocent III found in the Scriptures new arguments to demonstrate the universal vocation of the see of Rome and its pre-eminence over all Churches. As circumstances permitted, he prosecuted the work of centralization to the profit of the papacy. He realized that an overhaul of the administration was necessitated by the increasing complexity of its functions, so he reorganized the chancellery; in the specialization of its staff of notaries, scribes, correctors and bull-writers, and in its attention to detail it was appreciably ahead of the lay chancelleries. But, while intervening in the election of bishops and the conferring of benefices, and while seeking to augment his financial resources, he was not unmindful of the shafts that St Bernard had let fly at the Holy See: he did away with luxury at his court, he agreed to appeals to arbitrate only where it was necessary, the established powers of supervision he left to the metropolitans, rather than transfer them to legates.

In other matters, too, Innocent III knew how to listen to the aspirations of the mass of the faithful and give them expression. Indifference to worldly pleasures might be turned into a disinterested devotion to the unfortunate. Having approved the statutes of the congregation of hospitallers set up by Guy of Montpellier, the pope besought him to open a hospice in Rome: the Hospitallers of the Holy Ghost went on to establish charitable foundations throughout the West, staffed by lay brothers to whom, later, priests acted as chaplains. Innocent III also confirmed the Trinitarians (the Order of the Holy Trinity and of the Ransom of Captives), founded by the Provençal Jean de Matha, whose friars, clothed in a white mantle with a blue and red cross, riding donkeys, collected in Europe the money that they used in North Africa to free Christians captured by the Muslims.

Even so, as the opportunities to grow rich became more numerous, the desire for poverty animated an increasing number of hearts. The success of the heretics could be explained on these grounds; it was all too easy for them to denounce the wealth of the Church. As soon as they confessed the dogmas of the Roman Church, Innocent III authorized the Humiliati of Lombardy—formerly condemned by Lucius III—and the Poor Catholics of the former Waldensian Durand of Huesca to lead the life of austerity and mortification they had at first practised outside the law. He did not even forbid them to preach—for was not poverty the best assurance of a preacher's credentials, provided that his teaching was rigorously orthodox? To bring back the straying sheep, the pope first thought of the Cistercians, in whom "a saintly life is joined to right thinking and so quickens doctrine ... that men can read in their lives what their speech expounds"; but although they wore the same habit as St Bernard, his sons were not fired by the same apostolic zeal; they made little impression on Languedoc and its Cathar heresy. So Innocent III brought to bear on this region the efforts of Diego, the Spanish Bishop of Osma, and the subprior of his chapter, Dominic Guzman, when they desired to evangelize the regions of the Dniepr and the Lower Volga. On November 19th, 1206, the pope painted a picture of the new missionaries as "men of tried virtue, imitating the poverty of Christ, the Greatest of the Poor, not fearing to seek out, clad in humble clothing and with fiery breath, the heretics so as to rescue them from error, with the grace of God, through the example of their life and the skill of their speech"; he allowed them to live on alms alone, although under canon law clerks and monks were forbidden to beg.

In 1210 there came to him Francesco Bernardone of Assisi, and twelve companions, who explained to him that they had abandoned all their possessions; in the grey habit of penitents they were going through the countryside bringing news of the Gospels; they lived on public charity, repaired chapels and slept in huts, barns or caves. Did the head of the Church, when, as legend has it, he saw St Francis in a dream holding up the Lateran, have a revelation of the forces that this brotherly community of paupers was putting at his disposal? He gave Francis permission to preach the moral precepts of the Gospel and the faculty of renewing this authorization for each of his brothers.

When Innocent III thus placed under the protection of the Holy See two clearly very bold projects, from which were to spring the Order of Preachers (Dominicans) and that of the Friars Minor (Franciscans), he was not unaware that proper preaching must be prepared by the acquisition of a solid culture if it was not to deviate rapidly into personal and heterodox interpretations of the faith. He had to remind St Francis of this, whereas with St Dominic he found immediate agreement on the necessity for theological studies. In a good many places schools were flourishing, and speculation was developing. Lothair Conti had himself profited from the teaching at Paris and ‘Bologna. He was of the opinion that the Holy See ought to make its mark on the intellectual movement of the day and encourage it, but reserve the possibility of supervising it closely. He it was who watched over the early stages of "the university of masters and scholars of Paris", where teachers and students, established on the Ile de la Cité, on the narrow bridge joining the island to the left bank of the river and on the gentle slopes of "la montagne Sainte-Geneviève", came under several jurisdictions, including the irksome one of the chancellor of the cathedral chapter. They united among themselves, and we learn from a papal Bull of 1208 or 1209 that the masters had set up a commission to establish a statute to which everyone should conform; in 1212 and 1213, the pope limited the chancellor's prerogatives in the conferring of the licence (*licentia docendi*); finally his legate, Robert of Courçon, published the university statutes fixing the order, the timetable and the syllabuses of study, the discipline of students and even practical details like dress and the price of lodgings. In 1214 a cardinal had granted a charter of privileges to the community of masters and scholars of Oxford.

This control by the pope over the Church and all aspects of religious life received signal confirmation at the fourth Lateran Council. In November of 1215, 500 archbishops and bishops, 800 abbots and priors, as well as the delegates of chapters and the envoys of princes, met under the presidency of Pope Innocent III; it is probable that they worked on texts prepared in advance by the papal court; the seventy canons that they drew up, and that were immediately incorporated into the body of canon law, concerned dogma, morals, the hierarchy, benefices, the reform of the clergy and relations with lay authorities. Even so, at this general session of the Church where the doctrine of papal supremacy had been reaffirmed, the pope had spoken of the empire, the kingdom of England, the seigniories of Languedoc—in fine, of the temporal questions over which, as the leader of Christendom, he felt himself able to exercise a supervisory right.

THE STRUGGLE AGAINST THE ENEMIES OF THE ROMAN FAITH

Innocent III aimed both to recapture Jerusalem and destroy the heretics—that is, to continue the collective work of Christian society that Henry VI had very nearly arrogated to himself; as this amounted to rooting out the worst canker that can consume a religious society he had mobilized the temporal powers. But he did not always succeed in remaining master of the execution of his two projects.

There can be no doubt that the resumption of the crusade was one of his major objectives: it occupied his mind from his accession and he did not hesitate to assert his authority with the princes in order to realize it. The sovereigns did not respond, but at the call of preachers accredited by the pope, like Fulk of Neuilly, many of the barons of France, southern Germany and northern Italy took the cross. Innocent would have liked to assemble them in the kingdom of Sicily, which was a fief of the Roman Church. But once the army was raised the initiative passed from the pope's hands. The barons came to terms with the Venetians over transport; they decided to land in Egypt; by way of payment to their Venetian creditors, whom they were unable to pay in other coin, they undertook to recapture Zara, on the Dalmatian coast, which had been lost to the King of Hungary, then they fell prey to the promises of Alexius Angelus, whose father had been driven from the throne of Byzantium and who was hand in glove with Venice—avid to regain her privileged trading position in the eastern empire— and with Boniface of Montferrat, the military leader of the crusade. Innocent III was lavish with rebukes, warnings and threats of excommunication. But the crusaders made for Constantinople, re-established the Angeli, and eventually themselves took possession of the city on April 12th, 1204. As emperor they elected Baldwin, Count of Flanders.

It was useless then looking to the knights, now wholly en-grossed with their spoils, for the succouring of the Holy Land. Nevertheless, the idea of a pilgrimage of redemption was still alive among the masses; in 1212 there was a sudden movement among children in the Vendôme and Cologne areas. One can-not help wondering what was the mystical hope that fired them and caused their parents to consent to such a venture. Most of them fell off by the wayside; others, having sailed from Mar-seilles, were sold in the slave-markets of Africa; a few showed up in Rome to ask for absolution from the pope. But the pity and the pathos of their adventure constituted an ominous call to order. Innocent III was sensitive enough to popular feeling to understand this. He did not rest until a new expedition was prepared. The Lateran Council of 1215, called in part for this purpose, set one on foot, with detailed provision made for its recruitment, financing and concentration. But Innocent died in 1216, before the time fixed for its departure. He had never-theless been witness to a great victory over Islam: since he had supported the Archbishop of Toledo, Rodrigo Jimenez de Rada, in his efforts at propaganda and recruitment, he could take some credit for the success of Las Navas de Tolosa, in 1212, which made certain of the future of Christianity in the Iberian peninsula.

However bloody and scandalous it had been, the taking of Constantinople had at least one thing to be said for it: it per-mitted a Latin emperor and patriarch to be installed in the East. But was it not a deceptive benefit, more than offset by the hatred of the Greeks for the victors who had given themselves up to violence and were shamelessly despoiling the local clergy of their possessions? Innocent III tried to resolve the problem of the union of the two Churches in a spirit of moderation: he subordinated the patriarchate of Constantinople to himself and promoted the introduction of western prelates, clergy and monks into the eastern Church so as to instruct it in Roman customs and beliefs, but as soon as the authority of his see was recognized, he showed himself disposed to leave the Greek bishops in office; he was also prepared to admit certain rites peculiar to the eastern Church. These efforts failed: fragments of the empire had remained independent in Epirus and to the south of the Black Sea, where a new Greek patriarch had established himself at Nicaea; the Byzantine clergy in Romania (the name for the Latin empire in the East) looked to him alone. Conferences were arranged without success between representatives of the pope and those of the "Emperor of Nicaea". The council of 1215 might declare, "in our day the Greeks have returned to the apostolic obedience"; it was confusing a military victory—which in any case was precarious— with a religious conversion which was becoming increasingly contingent.

The crusade had degenerated into a war against Byzantium, with which was combined the object of reducing the heretics. From Bosnia to the basin of the Garonne, sects proliferated. The pope, as we have seen, aided the return to the fold of a few small groups and put his hope in preaching campaigns. He reminded the bishops of their duty to track down and condemn the opponents of the faith; he himself acted with vigour in his own states of central Italy. But of what use were these methods in Bosnia and Languedoc, where heresy was organized along the lines of a Church, was protected by the barons, viewed with sympathy by the people and strengthened by the mediocrity of the Catholic clergy? Dominic's triumph in a few disputations, the conversion of nine women who had previously been members of a group of the Perfect and were now accommodated in the convent of Prouille—these amounted to little.

Recourse to the secular arm was provided for in law, since the ecclesiastical authorities could apply only spiritual penalties. But Innocent III did not hesitate to extend their use to include war, which he endowed with the same privileges as the crusade. He set the King of Hungary against the principality of Bosnia; its head gave in. After the murder of the legate, Peter of Castelnau, by a serjeant of the Count of Toulouse, he pronounced sentence against Raymond VI: "We, according to the holy canons, by which fidelity is not owed to him who is not faithful to God, free from their oaths, as of our apostolic authority, all those who have sworn him fidelity, cooperation or alliance, and, the chief lord's rights being reserved, we give licence to all Catholics to proceed against his person, and even to occupy and hold his land." The volunteers were guaranteed the protection of the Holy See, the remission of debts and the absolution of sins.

"The Albigensian crusade" began in the early summer of 1209. It was no longer within the pope's power to do away with its excesses, nor to adopt a sympathetic attitude towards the Count of Toulouse, who was showing signs of wanting to make up for his indulgence toward heresy. The crusaders hacked a bloody path for themselves across the viscountcy of Béziers and Carcassonne, which they made over to one of the fieriest of their number, an unimportant baron from the Ile-de-France, Simon de Montfort. There were burnings at the stake; new bishops were appointed to the sees of southern France; knights from the north installed themselves. Supported by the legates, recognized by the Lateran Council and accepted by the suzerain—the King of France—Simon de Montfort became Count of Toulouse.

Whether the political upheavals effected in the name of the faith caused the heresy to vanish is another question. In fact they were no more effective than the installation of the Latins at Constantinople. The Bogomile churches of Bosnia waited patiently till a new prince should show them favour, when they would again hold their services openly. New forms had to be found for the inquisition so as to hunt down the Cathars of Languedoc. The Montforts did not even hold on to their conquest: they were harried by Raymond VII, the son of their victim, and made over their rights to the French king who set himself up in a part of the former county of Toulouse, before eventually absorbing it completely.

ITALY AND THE EMPIRE

Meanwhile, in order to be free to lay down the temporal objectives which the Christian princes should seek, Innocent III had to eliminate pressure and competition from the empire.

Henry VI had brought an intolerable threat to bear on the little papal states, and had clearly been bending his efforts towards the acquisition of a universal superiority. His premature death was fortunate for Innocent, especially as he left only a three-year-old son, Frederick Roger; his widow, to make sure that the kingdom of Sicily would pass to the child, hastened to recognize the papal suzerainty, of a century-and-a-half's standing, and since she herself died no later than the month of November, 1198, the boy king came under the guardianship of the pope, who exercised his right of seigniorial protection over the fief of an heir not yet of age. The whole of central Italy, moreover, arose to shake off the heavy hand of the Germanic administration. And in Germany the electors were divided between a brother of the dead emperor, Philip of Swabia, and Otto of Brunswick, both of whom managed to have themselves crowned. This turning of the tables allowed the pope to manoeuvre in the best interests of the Holy See and to emphasize a number of principles that were complementary to the theological arguments.

He applied himself, as a dutiful lord, to the protection and guidance of the young Frederick: he spared no efforts to keep him from the clutches of the former companions of Henry VI and a nationalist party. When he had succeeded, he called a parliament and himself reorganized southern Italy; then he declared the king of age and married him in 1209 to a princess of the house of Aragon, entirely devoted to the Church of Rome.

Over the rest of the peninsula, for which he cherished a fatherly affection, he would have liked to pose as a protector, anxious to watch over it with a particular care. In the midst of the bitter rivalries between cities and domains, which were scarcely ready to welcome the idea of national solidarity, he endeavoured at least to spread the conviction that his policy tended to dissipate the "clouds of adversity" that obscured the future of Italy. His immediate plan was to prevent a return to power of the imperial faction and protect the independence of the papacy, which he had seen to be so precarious under his predecessors. He succeeded, not without provoking some disturbances, in establishing his authority over Rome, whose senator he chose. He placed his own relatives in a few strategic points of St Peter's patrimony; above all he made sizeable additions to it. The states of the Church were reduced to a strip of territory, bounded by the sea and the mountains, lying on either side of the lower valley of the Tiber. The gifts of emperors since Carolingian times gave it a very much greater area: Innocent III used this as an argument for carrying out what his officials termed "recuperations"; he was able to install his rectors in the duchy of Spoleto and the march of Ancona, and to win a few fortified towns in the north of the patrimony. True, his claims in Tuscany and the Romagna came to nothing, nor was the power of his agents everywhere recognized, but thanks to him the see of Rome found itself at the head of a territory running slantwise across the peninsula from the Tyrrhenian to the Adriatic. He imbued ecclesiastical circles with the conviction that a considerable territorial base was necessary to the papacy for the free exercise of its spiritual leadership— and what complications, what shabby expedients, in the course of ages (down to the Lateran agreements of 1929) were to proceed from this idea?

The claims on his attention of Italy were too insistent for Innocent to occupy himself immediately with German affairs. He waited to be appealed to, but he proclaimed unequivocally that such recourse to him was indispensable. In January, 1201, in a "deliberation" in which he considered by turn what was right, what was expedient and what was profitable for the Holy See, he inclined to support, among the claimants to the throne, Otto of Brunswick. In the decretal *Venerabilem* he explained that he was not opposed to the electoral rights of the German princes, as the civil power had its sphere of autonomy, but that he had good grounds for intervening since, historically, it was the papacy that had handed on the empire from the Greeks to the Franks, and then to the Germans, and that the emperor must be worthy of serving the Christian cause. Innocent took action on behalf of his candidate with the German princes and prelates; he received him at Rome in 1209. Shoulders covered by the red mantle that Pope Sylvester had received from Constantine, head crowned with the tiara signifying the supreme authority vested only in the Vicar of Christ, he sat before the *confessio* of St Peter; after the introit, Otto had been anointed by cardinals; Innocent III invested him with the crown, the sceptre and the sword. "Receive this sword", he said, "taken by our hands from the body of the Blessed Peter and imperially granted to you for the defence of the Holy Church of God." The ceremonial, for once, really did correspond with the political reality.

This happy state of affairs was short-lived. Otto IV set about restoring the imperial power in Italy; he reoccupied towns and invaded the kingdom of Sicily. By November 18th, 1210, the pope was obliged to excommunicate him, and the following year to support the election as king of Frederick of Sicily, who had been recommended to the electors of Germany by the King of France. Although Henry VI's son had been his own ward, Innocent took every precaution to see that the father's plans were not revived: he received afresh homage and the oath of loyalty for the kingdom of Sicily; he demanded the renunciation of the lands in the centre of the peninsula that he had recently annexed; he obtained the surrender of the privileges that the Concordat of Worms had left to the ruler of Germany; he made the young man promise that, once crowned emperor, he would no longer govern Sicily but would make it over to his son; and he enlisted him in the crusade that was about to be organized. The man who, after Otto's defeat at Bouvines,

had imposed himself as master of Germany appeared to be
the faithful servant of the papacy.

THE POPE AND THE KINGS OF EUROPE

The empire was in a unique position: it affected a power
that was capable of being extended to an extraordinary degree,
and in the last resort the whole organization of Christendom.
It was not necessary, in other cases, for the pope to have a
finger in every pie, on the pretext that the priestly power was
superior to all others.

Did the lord of Montpellier wish to legitimize his bastards?
then let him go to his overlord. There was a feudal hierarchy,
with its own customs; the pope did not interfere with it; he
would only take the initiative in cases where no secular
authority was there to resolve the question. Once this principle
was established, the pontiff was responsible for promoting
morality, justice and peace, and defending the freedom of the
Church. The King of Leon had married a cousin without obtaining a dispensation; Philip Augustus of France had found
prelates complaisant enough to annul his marriage with Inge-
borg of Denmark, and had taken to wife his cousin, Agnes of
Méran. These were clear infringements of canon law. As the
kingly dignity cannot take precedence over the duties of a
Christian, the pope announced their excommunication and put
an interdict on their domains. Philip Augustus refused to call
a halt to the hostilities he had embarked on against the King
of England, whose fiefs he had sentenced to confiscation: the
truce that the two men had sworn had been broken; a matter
of the common good, higher in kind than an ordinary feudal
dispute, was at stake; the moral law was being flouted; since
there was sin, he who had the power of binding and loosing
had the right himself to intervene in the political order. King
John had forced his candidate on the see of Canterbury; Innocent had nominated Stephen Langton to it. The king had refused to accept him, and what is more was putting his hands

on church property and persecuting the clergy who opposed him. The pope put England under an interdict, excommunicated John, released his subjects from their duty of loyalty and his allies from that of honouring their treaties. He commissioned the French king to seize the kingdom of an unworthy sovereign. John saw that he was lost: he swore to obey the pope and on May 15th, 1213, declared that henceforth he would no longer hold his kingdom save as a fief of the Roman Church, and would pay an annual tribute.

Innocent III, who bound new schools and congregations directly to the Holy See by virtue of the ancient practice of exemption, was fond of fashioning special ties of subordination between the papacy and the princes. He probably had no intention of reducing all the states of Christendom to the status of vassals, but he found in the social patterns of his day a convenient method of having his prerogatives respected. In his relations with Sicily—as we have seen—he conducted himself as a true suzerain; and also with England, since he set aside the famous Magna Carta of 1215 that the rebel barons had wrested, under constraint and without his agreement, from his vassal John. More commonly, the undertakings entered into by the princes allowed for the more efficient protection of the privileges of the Church; these were the lines on which ran the oath sworn by the King of Aragon when he came to Rome, and the recommendations that the pontiff addressed to the kings of Hungary. And in conferring the title "royal" on a Walachian prince who had mastered Bulgaria, Innocent III was not blind to the profit of bringing into the Roman obedience a Church taken from Greek influence.

When all is said and done, from the county of Toulouse to the Latin empire of Constantinople, from England to the Iberian peninsula and Italy, the pope had brought into being ties of dependency. With him Christendom had taken on a markedly organic character: the Holy See was judge of its interests and of its title to ordain the temporal acts in which the kings must concur. The priest's authority had passed from the intimate field of conscience to that of public law. It did not do away with the competence and autonomy of the lay power, but it surpassed them; Christian society, in the hierarchical form it had assumed, was pursuing the common weal and constituted in the world a force distinct from the Church but guided by the Church. The value of Innocent III's pontificate lies in the fact that such statements as these were not merely the formulas of theorists or the reconstitutions of historians, but approximated to the living reality.

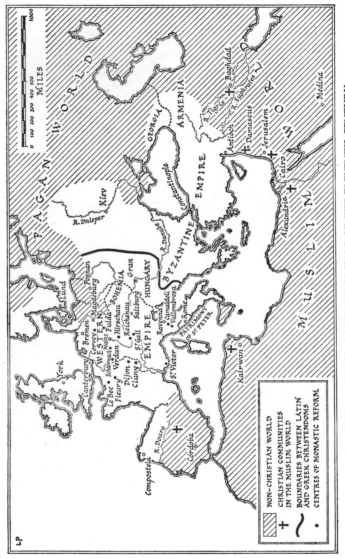

THE CHRISTIAN WORLD IN THE FIRST HALF OF THE ELEVENTH CENTURY

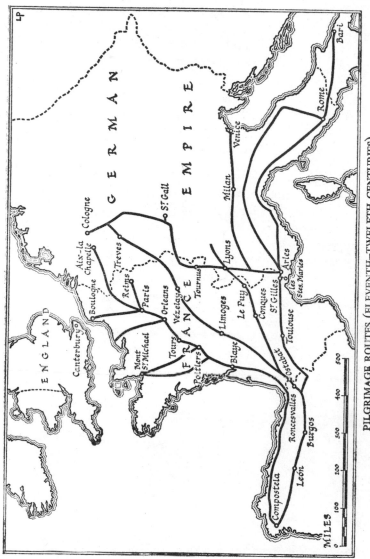

PILGRIMAGE ROUTES (ELEVENTH–TWELFTH CENTURIES)

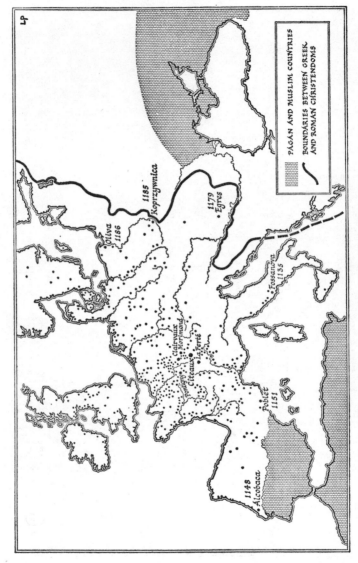

GROWTH OF THE CISTERCIAN ORDER

PAGAN AND MUSLIM COUNTRIES

BOUNDARIES BETWEEN GREEK
AND ROMAN CHRISTENDOMS

1185
Koprzywnica

1179
Eqres

Oliva
1186

Fossanova
1155

Clairvaux
Morimond
Pontigny La Ferté
Cîteaux

Poblet
1151

Alcobaça
1148

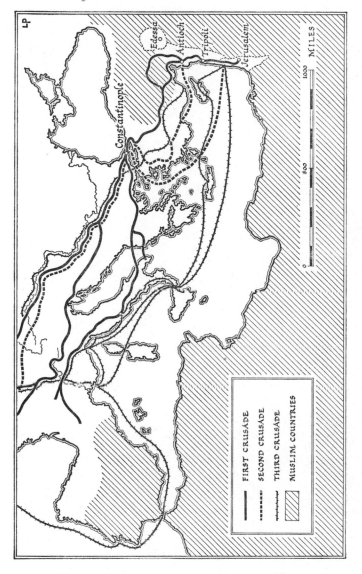

CRUSADE ROUTES (END ELEVENTH–TWELFTH CENTURY)

LP

ICELAND

Uppsala
Abo
ESTHONIA
LIVONIA
RUSSIANS
Lund
Riga
PRUSSIA
LITHUANIA
ENGLAND
Hamburg
Cammin
POLAND
Oxford
CUMANS
Paris
FRANCE
EMPIRE
HUNGARY
LEÓN
Toulouse
Prouille
BOSNIA
Bologna
BULGARIA
Constantinople
Trebizond
NAVARRE
ARAGON
Assisi
Thessaly
CASTILE
PAPAL
STATES
Rome
KINGDOM
Nicaea
CHRISTIAN
KINGDOM
OF ARMENIA
PORTUGAL
Calatrava
Navas
de Tolosa
OF
Antioch
SICILY
CYPRUS
Acre
Jerusalem

Boundaries of Roman Christendom
Directions of Evangelization
ARAGON   Vassal states of the Roman Church
Latin states of the East
Remains of the Byzantine Empire
•   Universities recognized by Innocent III
Areas of heresies
★   First centres of mendicant orders

MILES
0   500

ROMAN CHRISTENDOM IN THE TIME OF INNOCENT III (1198–1216)

SELECT BIBLIOGRAPHY

Standard histories

The Cambridge Medieval History, volumes IV–VI, Cambridge and New York, Cambridge Univ. Press, 1911–36.

The Cambridge Economic History of Europe, two volumes, Cambridge and New York, Cambridge Univ. Press, 1941–52.

POOLE, A. L.: *From Domesday Book to Magna Carta* (volume III of *The Oxford History of England*), Oxford and New York, Oxford Univ. Press, 1951.

POWICKE, F. M.: *The Thirteenth Century* (volume IV of *The Oxford History of England*), Oxford and New York, Oxford Univ. Press, 1953.

General or ecclesiastical history

BARRACLOUGH, G.: *Medieval Germany*, two volumes, Oxford and New York, Oxford Univ. Press, 1938.

BOISSONADE, P.: *Life and Work in Medieval Europe*, translated E. Power, London, Kegan Paul, New York, Knopf, 1937.

DAWSON, Christopher: *Religion and the Rise of Western Culture*, London and New York, Sheed and Ward, 1950.

HASKINS, C. H.: *The Renaissance of the Twelfth Century*, Oxford, Oxford Univ. Press, and Cambridge, Mass., Harvard Univ. Press, 1927; reprint, New York, Meridian Books, 1957.

HUGHES, P.: *A History of the Church*, volume II, *The Church and the World the Church Created*, 2nd edn, London and New York, Sheed and Ward, 1948.

JAMES, Bruno Scott: *Saint Bernard of Clairvaux*, London, Hodder and Stoughton, and New York, Harper, 1957.

OSTROGORSKY, G.: *History of the Byzantine State*, translated J. Hussey, Oxford, Blackwell, 1956, and New Brunswick, N.J., Rutgers Univ. Press, 1957.

OTTO, Bp of Freising: *The Deeds of Frederick Barbarossa*, translated C. C. Mierow, New York, Columbia Univ. Press, 1953.

PIRENNE, H.: *Medieval Cities*, translated F. D. Halsey, Princeton, Princeton Univ. Press, 1925; *Economic and Social History of Medieval Europe*, translated I. E. Clegg, London, Kegan Paul, and New York, Harcourt, 1947.

RUNCIMAN, J. C. S.: *The Medieval Manichee*, Cambridge and New York, Cambridge Univ. Press, 1947; *A History of the Crusades*, Cambridge and New York, Cambridge Univ. Press, 1951–4; *The Eastern Schism*, Oxford and New York, Oxford Univ. Press, 1955.

SETTON, K. M. (editor): *A History of the Crusades*, volume I (others not yet published), Philadelphia, Univ. of Pennsylvania Press, 1955.

SMAIL, R. C.: *Crusading Warfare (1097–1197)*, Cambridge and New York, Cambridge Univ. Press, 1956.

SOUTHERN, R. W.: *The Making of the Middle Ages*, London, Hutchinson, and Newhaven, Conn., Yale Univ. Press, 1953.

STEPHENSON, C.: *Medieval Feudalism*, Ithaca, N.Y., Cornell Univ. Press, 1942.

TELLENBACH, G.: *Church, State and Christian Society at the Time of the Investiture Conflict*, translated R. F. Bennett, Oxford and New York, Oxford Univ. Press, 1940.

VASILIEV, A. A.: *History of the Byzantine Empire, 324–1453*, Oxford, Blackwell, and Madison, Univ. of Wisconsin Press, 1952.

Philosophy and Theology
In this series: CHENU, M. D., O.P.: *Is Theology a Science?* CRISTIANI, Léon: *Heresies and Heretics*; DELHAYE, Philippe: *Christian Philosophy in the Middle Ages.*

ARTZ, F. B.: *The Mind of the Middle Ages, 200–1500*, 2nd edn, New York, Knopf, 1954.

GILSON, Etienne H.: *The Spirit of Medieval Philosophy*, London and New York, Sheed and Ward, 1936 (reprint 1950); *The Mystical Theology of Saint Bernard*, London and New York, Sheed and Ward, 1940; *History of Christian Philosophy in the Middle Ages*, London, Sheed and Ward, 1955; *The Christian Philosophy of Saint Thomas Aquinas*, London, Gollancz, and New York, Random House, 1957.

LEFF, G.: *Medieval Thought from Saint Augustine to Ockham*, London and Baltimore, Penguin Books, 1958.

Art and Architecture
CONANT, K. J.: *Carolingian and Romanesque Architecture, 800–1200*, London and Baltimore, Penguin Books, 1959.

LETHABY, W. R.: *Medieval Art, 312–1350*, London and New York, Nelson, 1949.

PEVSNER, N.: *An Outline of European Architecture*, London and New York, Penguin Books, revised edn. 1945.

RICE, D. Talbot: *Byzantine Art*, Oxford and New York, Oxford Univ. Press, 1935.